Birthright

Sis-hu-lk

Birthright

Constance Lindsay Skinner

adapted by Joan Bryans
introduction by Jean Barman
afterword by Michelle La Flamme

Playwrights Canada Press
Toronto • Canada

The Birthright © Copyright 1906 Constance Lindsay Skinner
Birthright (adaptation) © Copyright 2003 Joan Bryans
Introduction © Copyright 2005 Jean Barman
Afterword "Blood Will Tell" © Copyright 2005 Michelle La Flamme
The moral rights of the authors are asserted.

Playwrights Canada Press
The Canadian Drama Publisher
215 Spadina Avenue, Suite 230, Toronto, Ontario CANADA M5T 2C7
416-703-0013   fax 416-408-3402
orders@playwrightscanada.com • www.playwrightscanada.com

Financial support provided by the taxpayers of Canada and Ontario through the Canada Council for the Arts and the Department of Canadian Heritage through the Book Publishing Industry Development Programme, and the Ontario Arts Council.

The Canada Council for the Arts
Le Conseil des Arts du Canada

ONTARIO ARTS COUNCIL
CONSEIL DES ARTS DE L'ONTARIO

Front cover painting "Indian Maiden" by Sis-hu-lk. Image courtesy of BC Archives.
Production Editor: JLArt

Library and Archives Canada Cataloguing in Publication

Skinner, Constance Lindsay, 1882-1939

    Birthright / Constance Lindsay Skinner ; adapted by Joan Bryans ; introduction by Jean Barman ; afterword by Michelle La Flamme.

Adaptation of the unpublished play, originally written 1906, first with the working title Aidzumka, and then as The birthright.

ISBN 0-88754-752-4

    1. Whites--Relations with Indians--Drama. 2. Métis--British Columbia--Drama.
3. Frontier and pioneer life--British Columbia--Drama.

I. Bryans, Joan, 1941- II. Title.

PS3537.K53B57 2005   C812'.52   C2005-905745-9

First edition: November 2005.
Printed and bound by AGMV Marquis at Quebec, Canada.

Acknowledgements

Thanks to:

Jean Barman for discovering Skinner's
work and sharing it with me.

M. Jane Smith for invaluable help on the Gitxsan
language and customs.

Andree Karas, United Players of Vancouver and the Jericho
Arts Centre for help in mounting the Canadian premiere.

Table of Contents

Constance Lindsay Skinner

Introduction

by Jean Barman

The Birthright, renamed *Birthright* in this adaptation, is about the resilience of the human spirit. [1] Written at the beginning of the twentieth century, the play looked to a future when Aboriginal people and the newcomers who usurped their land and their souls would find common ground. The protagonist, Precious Conroy, is unwilling to accept the equation of Aboriginal descent with racial inferiority. At the beginning of the play she is unaware of her "birthright," and she cannot conceive, on learning of her mixed-race parentage, that she is thereby any less a human being. Precious' attitude is completely at odds with the common justification for newcomers' actions, that Aboriginal people were incapable of looking after themselves.

The Birthright is also about the duplicity that as human beings we all practice from time to time. Precious' adoptive parents are missionaries on the British Columbia north coast. So long as they can see themselves as "doing good" toward Precious, they treat her as their own child. It is when she acts on the values of equality they have fostered in her, by returning the affection their biological son feels toward her, that the missionary couple turn on her. They are convinced that, once they reveal Precious' inheritance to her, she will internalise the inferiority they, as a matter of course, attribute to her. Precious sees no reason to do so, and the action of the play ensues.

The Birthright's plot is driven by the optimism of youth. The principal characters, apart from the missionary couple, believe in the possibility of change. Precious and their son are convinced, at least in the moment, that they can lead the lives they choose for themselves. So is the competitor for Precious' affections. Louis Prince, who is, like Precious, of mixed descent, considers that, by virtue of their common inheritance, the future is theirs to make.

The optimism emanates from *The Birthright's* author. Constance Lindsay Skinner wrote the play in her mid-twenties, convinced she could, like Precious, take on the world and come out the winner. Constance was born in 1877 in the British Columbia interior, where her father ran a Hudson's Bay fur trading post. A cosseted only child, Constance was eleven when the Skinners moved to Vancouver and she was enrolled in a private girls' school, which nourished her confidence to write.

The Birthright's plot line originated during these years. Much later in life, Constance reflected how "the only sister I ever had, the daughter of dear friends of my parents, who adopted her and brought her up with me, had Indian blood." Maggie Alexander's father was a Scots Hudson's Bay officer stationed near to where the Skinners had lived. Her half Aboriginal mother belonged to the legendary fur trade clan that descended from Peter Skene Ogden from Anglo-Quebec. In the parlance of the day, Maggie was a "quarter breed." Her mother's death and her father's desire that she grow up "with educated and refined people" were responsible for Maggie being sent to live with the Skinners and joining Constance in the private school she attended. The two girls grew close, so much so, "Connie would never get on without her." [2]

Maggie Alexander introduced Constance to the themes that animate *The Birthright*. As the play opens, Precious has just returned from a California private school, to which she, like Maggie, was sent to erase the stigma of her birth. In the view of the time, supported by a kind of pseudo-science, the civilising process could only be a veneer. It could not eradicate Maggie's and Precious' innate inferiority based in skin pigment. As Precious' adoptive mother puts it in the play, "no matter what one does, the wild blood will show itself." However small in proportion, Aboriginal descent was to be abhorred. Precious' blonde competitor for the missionary son's attention expresses the common wisdom when she exclaims, "Indian blood is Indian blood and the amount of it makes very little difference."

Aboriginal descent engaged Constance even while Maggie still lived with the Skinners. In her mid-teens Constance began contributing articles under a pseudonym to Vancouver newspapers. She often told the story of what happened when her "first work of fiction" turned up in a Sunday issue. "Considered risqué in those days," the article was about "the 'worser' whites mingling with the natives" along the coast. "With heart athrill she listened to a guarded discussion of it by her parents" and asked to see the paper. "'No,' said her mother kindly,... 'It is not the sort of thing I want you to read. You are far too young.'" [3]

By the time Constance reached her twenties, she was convinced Vancouver was a literary backwater and longed to escape. An illness in 1900 made it possible for her to do so. Sent to Los Angeles to stay with an aunt to recover, she never looked back. Constance talked her way into a job as drama and music critic for a Los Angeles newspaper. Within a couple of years she was one of publisher William Randolph Hearst's early "sob sisters," women journalists who used interviews with celebrities to disclose their innermost secrets in print.

Constance's literary ambitions were fired both by her job and by her bohemian life style. She took a room in the large rambling house of sculptor Jeanie Spring Peet, whose parents had been leading abolitionists and communitarians. Jeanie's son Cloudsley Johns described her as "a woman of extraordinary personality, not at all inclined toward unquestioning reverence for anything." He and his younger brother Herbert Heron were equally original in their thinking. Cloudsley was a pal of successful journalist and author Jack London, who admired the stability Constance brought to the erratic household. "Constance, you're a brick—a fine noble woman. About the noblest I've met in this vale of the world. Wolf." Like the others in the ménage, he encouraged Constance to write. In a Christmas poem Herbert had written for her, he evoked "the vision of your den... with the tables piled with pens, and golden manuscripts, and pens, and folded paper, and tobacco jars." In every way a "new woman," Constance not only smoked, she rolled her own cigarettes. Sunday evenings at 500 North Soto Street were given over to conversation, when a group of four or five engaged in "drifting talk" on topics ranging from "sacred history" to fashionable playwrights Henrik Ibsen and George Bernard Shaw. For Constance, Los Angeles was "a hot house for brains," where "feelings blaze and flourish like its poppy fields." [4]

Constance's confidence reinforced at every turn, she sought to make her mark as a playwright. She and Herbert Heron wrote five plays together, drawing on her experience as a drama critic and his as a sometimes actor. While none were successful, Constance had a couple of triumphs on her own before turning to the other genres— poetry, short stories, history, adult and juvenile novels—by which she would make her literary reputation. Shortly after Constance left Los Angeles for Chicago in 1908, moving to New York City in 1912, Herbert headed north to the artists' community of Carmel, near to where Jack London lived. There Herbert founded an outdoor amphitheatre whose opening production in January 1911 was Constance's biblical play, *David*, selected so he could play the lead. Six years later Constance's play about a rich young Anglo-Quebec widow finding love again, *Good Morning, Rosamond!*, opened to good reviews in one of the New York City theatres belonging to the Shubert brothers, the theatrical moguls of the day.

Constance pinned her hopes as a playwright on *The Birthright*. It was, Herbert Heron reminded her, "what you sentimentally call 'the first-fruits of my brain.'" She tried out the plot line in the newspaper story that scandalised her parents, in a short story called "Under the Shadow of the Pines (Tales of the West Coast of British Columbia)" that in 1899 she tried unsuccessfully to publish in Toronto, and in "The Home-Coming of Marie-Pierre," which appeared in the January-June 1903 issue of the Los Angeles magazine *Out West*. Then came the play, originally entitled *Aidzumka* and renamed *The Birthright* on Herbert's suggestion. Constance, who copyrighted the play in 1906, used every means at her disposal to get it staged. After interviewing the celebrated Shakespearean actress Helena Modjeska for a story in 1903, Constance assiduously cultivated the older woman. She persuaded her, while performing in New York City, to show *The Birthright* to producers who, according to Constance, considered it "a little too modern and also too daring in the handling of its original theme." In 1909 Constance negotiated with well-known producer David Belasco for a Los Angeles production, but nothing ensued. The next year Constance gave the rights, in exchange for 5 per cent of gross receipts, to J.J. Shubert for production in the Garrick Theatre in Chicago. "It will make a sensation because of its gripping drama and its novelty," Shubert is meant to have enthused. *The Birthright* played there and then in Boston in 1912. [5]

By now living in New York City, Constance set her sights on Broadway. Although announced for the 1912-13 season, *The Birthright* did not open. She kept chiding Shubert, who in March 1916 finally saw "an opportunity to produce the play." He engaged a cast for a fall opening at the Shubert Theatre on West 44th Street, but there was a catch. "It would have to be revised somewhat" to suit the female star, and Shubert proposed that her husband have "a free hand in making the adaptation" and, by virtue of doing so, garner half of Constance's royalties. She desisted, even though the husband had some years earlier written a hit play for Shubert, who now played hardball. "Evidently you do not care whether the play is produced or not.... Sometimes it is well to pocket a little pride and get a little money." Constance held firm, convinced that her reputation would suffer from the plot's alteration. Shubert's parting shot made clear every woman's difficulties attempting to enter what was still a man's world. "I think your arguments are all against you, but as you are of the feminine gender it is hardly necessary for me to try and convince you." So far as he was concerned, "it is mere obstinacy on your part not to allow us to go ahead." From Constance's perspective, far more was involved. She later reflected how "in 1916 Shubert offered me $250.00 & immediate production of a play of mine if I would put a certain decadent tint through the whole fabric of it; &, tho' I was up against the wall hard [for money], I turned it down without a regret." [6]

The Birthright seems to have had no further performances. It was, as Constance's experience makes clear, daring for the time. A play about the freedom to love openly and without shame, even across racial boundaries, might have been attuned to Constance's outlook and her way of life, but it was ahead of its time. As critic Roger Hall explains, while drama situated on the frontier was just gaining acceptance in mainstream theatres across North America in the early twentieth century, the outcomes of interracial romances tended to be sidestepped rather than confronted directly on the stage as in The Birthright. [7]

The Birthright's survival as a text is no less remarkable. Plays are by their nature ephemeral. The goal is not a piece of writing for posterity, but a stage production. At the time The Birthright was conceived, before the duplicating machine and the word processor, the usual practice was to type out a draft with as many carbons as were legible—five or six at the most—to send to prospective producers or lead actors and, possibly, to the copyright office. Any whiff of interest brought revisions intended to make the play more attractive that either were marked on an existing copy or incorporated into a new typed draft. In 1908 Herbert Heron lauded Constance for rewriting parts of The Birthright: "I'm glad you cut out [Chief] Kitsilano's scene. I never thought it was up to the rest of the play. You say Precious has more of the audience's sympathy, now. That is also good. And more Louis Prince is an improvement. Bully for you!" A year later he chided Constance for requesting his copy back, "Haven't you your own copy of the revised Birthright? You're foolish if you haven't." [8] A play's production entailed yet more changes. Except for the successes, final, published versions of plays from this time period are rare.

The Birthright survived for two reasons. First, it was particularly dear to its author, who all her life retained the hope it would enjoy the success she was convinced it deserved. Second, at Constance Lindsay Skinner's sudden death without a will in 1939, her publisher scooped up all her papers from her Manhattan apartment, including several iterations of *The Birthright*. Constance was sufficiently well-known on the American literary scene for her papers to be lodged in the Rare Books and Manuscript Division of the New York Public Library, where they remain to the present day. The version of *The Birthright* that is adapted here is the one that, from internal evidence, appears to be the most complete.

It would only be in 2003, thanks to the skillful adaptation of Vancouver director Joan Bryans with the assistance of Gitxsan playwright M. Jane Smith, that *The Birthright* was revived. Keeping the action at the beginning of the twentieth century and staying faithful to the author's style, Bryans updated the language and streamlined the action by cutting out scenes and characters extraneous to the plot line. Renamed *Birthright* to distinguish it from the original, the play had a successful two-week run in Vancouver in May 2003. Constance Lindsay Skinner would have been pleased that the Aboriginal roles— five out of ten—were played by Aboriginal actors and that *Birthright* was embraced by British Columbians of every age and background. The issues the play confronts still resonate a century after it was conceived. Attitudes have changed tremendously, but not entirely so. *Birthright* reminds us where we have been and also where we want to head.

Endnotes

1 This introduction draws from Jean Barman, *Constance Lindsay Skinner: Writing on the Frontier* (Toronto: University of Toronto Press, 2002); and Jean Barman, "'Vancouver's First Playwright': Constance Lindsay Skinner and *The Birthright*," *BC Studies: The British Columbian Quarterly* 137 (Spring 2003), 47-61. The introduction is also informed by the correspondence between Constance Lindsay Skinner [CLS] and Herbert Heron [HH], 1906-21, in the Harrison Memorial Library, Carmel, California. I am grateful to California writer Paul Hershey for alerting me to the correspondence on reading the biography and to Denise Sallee for making it available to us.

2 CLS to Annie Laurie Williams, NY, June 30, 1938; Alexander Lindsay to Annie Skinner, Fort Simpson, August 19, 1890, and enclosure; Henry Edwardes to Annie Skinner, Magila, Zanzibar, October 30, 1891, all in Skinner Papers, New York Public Library [NYPL]. For the index, see http://www.nypl.org/research/chss/spe/rbk/faids/skinner.html

3 "Woman Debunks the Northwest." *Brooklyn Eagle,* n.d. [March 1929], NYPL.

4 Cloudsley Johns, "Who the Hell is Cloudsley Johns?" 38, typescript in Huntington Library; Jack London to CLS, Sonoma County, 31 October 1906; HH, "Runes of Memory," Christmas 1908, typescript, NYPL; CLS, "Our Debt to the Actor," *New York Dramatic Mirror,* January 15, 1913.

5 HH to CLS, Sea Girt, NJ, March 23, 1911, Harrison Memorial Library; "Chicago Has a New Drama," *Chicago Evening American,* n.d; contract with John H. Blackwood, Belasco Theater, Los Angeles, March 22, 1909; contract with J.J. Shubert, August 2, 1910, all NYPL.

6 "Boston to See 'Birthright,'" *Sunday Boston American,* August 25, 1912; [CLS] "Plays and Players by a First Nighter," *Ainslee's* 30, 4 (November 1912): 155; J.J. Shubert to CLS, New York, March 12, 27, 29, April 6, 1916, NYPL; CLS to Vilhjlmer Stefansson, New York, September 11, 1923, Stefansson Papers, Dartmouth College Library.

7 Roger A. Hall, *Performing the American Frontier, 1870-1906* (Cambridge: Cambridge University Press, 2001), 199-234.

Previously, Aboriginality was objectified on the stage, as with Buffalo Bill Cody's Wild West shows and Canadian poet Pauline Johnson's performances, or vilified in vaudeville and melodrama. I am grateful to Christian Bock, who is completing a PhD dissertation at the Universität Osnabrück on the history of Canadian women playwrights, for his perceptive insights.

[8] HH to CLS, Los Angeles, August 26, 1908, Carmel, April 30, 1909, Harrison Memorial Library. This paragraph is based on their extensive correspondence.

The Adaptation of Skinner's *Birthright*

by Joan Bryans

When we had the first read-through of this newly discovered play we were stunned by how vibrant and relevant, not to mention beautiful, Skinner's work was. But it was also clear that in order for Skinner's work to come across to a modern audience an adaptation was necessary.

There were practical considerations to be sure, but there were also more serious matters. We doubted that even the most forgiving and understanding of audiences could get past some of the inappropriate language and Hollywood-like depictions of Native practices and lore in order to appreciate her work.

But here I was, a white woman, attempting to remedy the situation. The endeavour was a cultural minefield! The problem was resolved when the pre-eminent Gitxsan scholar and storyteller M. Jane Smith came to my aid. Her help and advice gave me the support and clarity necessary to proceed. [1]

Some problems were simply reflective of the theatrical style of the times: an irritating habit of having the addressee's name in almost every sentence uttered; a host of Native characters who appear in a scene as background set dressing, saying little, and never appear again.

But these were minor compared with the problems surrounding Skinner's use of language describing or being used by the Native characters. Firstly, the English words once used in ordinary conversation to describe Aboriginals and their way of life are insulting and demeaning today. It is one thing to have an evil or prejudiced character say those words—the audience can dismiss them as a reflection of that character. It is quite another when a hero or heroine mouths them to describe themselves or their people. To modern ears it seems as if the character is being self-denigrating, putting down their own folk, when in fact they are merely using what they take to be a neutral word.

Secondly, it would seem that Skinner, though very knowledgeable about Native practices and sensitivities of the time, lacked any knowledge of a Native language which she could put in the mouths of her characters. So, as Hollywood would later decide to do, she just made one up! In the adaptation Gitxsan has been used.

Again, in the lyric passages, Skinner at times embellishes her knowledge of Native practices and beliefs with a romantic hue—no harm in that—but she also invents Gods and sacred ceremonies to jazz it up. Clearly care had to be taken there to tread between the rocks of cultural misappropriation and the beauty of Skinner's lyric poetry.

All in all the adaptation was done with a very light hand: it was not my desire to rewrite the play. Nor was there any need. My aim in such alterations and in all the other small matters involved in the adaptation has been first and foremost to clear the way of any unnecessary distractions and to allow Skinner's work to speak directly to a modern audience.

Endnote

[1] Jane's recent book, *Returning the Feathers: Five Gitxsan Stories*, is published by Creekstone Press (Smithers, B.C.), 2004.

Production Information

The original Canadian production of Constance Lindsay Skinner's *Birthright* (using this adaptation) was a co-production between Vital Spark theatre and United Players of Vancouver in May 2003, with the following artistic team.

Precious Conroy	Odessa Shuquaya
Louis Prince (Hlaagoo't)	Jason Krowe
Harry Maclean	Adam Lolacher
Rev. Robert Maclean	Bob Rathie
Mrs. Martha Maclean	Annie Smith
Sim'oogit	Duane Howard
Conroy	Terrence Loychuk
Mrs. Redfern	Fran Burnside
Cissie Redfern	Katie Murphy
Mary / Koksilah	Beverley Machelle
Original music	Mark Germani
Flute	Duane Howard
Gitxsan songs	Angie Coombs
Gitxsan storyteller	
(voice-over)	Jane Smith Mowatt
Statue	Randy Fielding
Director	Joan Bryans
Fight Director	Sebastien de Castell
Stage Manager	Claudine Parker
Set Design	John R. Taylor
Lighting Design	Darren W. Hales
Costume Design	Tanya Seltenrich
Sound Design	Glenn Jamison
Properties	Frances Herzer
Photographer	Chris LeMay
Graphic Design	Val Kan & Randy Plett
Program	Sandi McDonald

Characters

Reverend Robert Maclean	a missionary
Mrs. Martha Maclean	his wife
Harold (Harry) Maclean	their son
Precious Conroy	their adopted daughter
Mrs. Redfern	friend of the Macleans
Cissie Redfern	her daughter
Sim'oogit	Indian tribal chief
Louis Prince (Hlaagoo't)	his son
Tom Conroy	cousin of Mrs. Maclean
Koksilah*	Young wife of Sim'oogit
Mary*	Indian housemaid of the Macleans

* can be played by same actor

Setting

Naas River, British Columbia. Midsummer, 1905. The action of the play occurs over a period of three days.

Act I   The drawing room of the Reverend Maclean's house.
Act II   In the village, outside the church.
Act III As Act I.
Act IV   In the nearby forest.

BIRTHRIGHT

Act I

Drawing room of the Maclean house in Northwestern British Columbia. Comfortably but not artistically furnished. DR there is a door to MACLEAN's study. Up are wide French doors which open onto a veranda, off which a trail leads through the forest. Mountains are seen in the distance. A half life-sized clay statue wrapped in cloth is on a turntable with modelling tools nearby.

It is mid afternoon, midsummer. Sun slants in, making the forest beyond seem very dark.

LOUIS Prince enters from veranda and wanders around room (suspiciously? is he up to no good?), picking up objects. MARY enters with tea tray. LOUIS is startled by her entrance, putting down an object quickly.

MARY   Hey, Louis Prince. What-for-you-come?

She goes to tea table and puts down tea tray.

LOUIS   I-got-table for Miss Conroy.

MARY   Huh! Put him over dere!

LOUIS   Where Miss Conroy?

MARY   Huh! She go walk.

MRS. MACLEAN   (*off-stage*) Mary, have you set the cups out for afternoon tea? I expect the cannery people today!

MARY   Yes, M's Mac-Lean.

LOUIS   What way Miss Conroy go?

MARY   Huh, in wood!

LOUIS   What road she go?

MARY   Up-dere-back-of-house. What you care?

> *LOUIS exits quickly as MRS. MACLEAN enters, corrects MARY's setting of tea things.*

MRS. MACLEAN   Watch the biscuits in the oven, Mary. (*MARY exits. Mrs. MACLEAN refers to the statue:*) It is simply dreadful—so disheartening. (*as MACLEAN enters*) Oh Robert, I was going to call you. I want to talk to you.

MACLEAN   Yes?

MRS. MACLEAN   It's about Precious.

MACLEAN   Ah—about Precious.

MRS. MACLEAN   Yes. I'm, afraid we have made a serious mistake—

MACLEAN   A mistake?

MRS. MACLEAN   I mean—her being away from us all these years. Of course I know Ida could never have made the marriage she has if Precious had been with us—but—

MACLEAN   There is no question of the wisdom of what we did. We would seriously have jeopardised Ida's future if we had brought up Precious in our home where her antecedents were known.

MRS. MACLEAN   I know that but, oh Robert, the girl is hardly a Christian. Have you seen that last—er—figure—statue—the one she has been so unwilling to talk about? It's over there!

MACLEAN   In here?

MRS. MACLEAN   Yes! She and Louis Prince brought it down today. She said something about the light in this room being best—

> *MACLEAN crosses to statue, takes off cloth, discloses a half-draped figure of woman sitting on a rock. One hand keeps the drape up, the other holds California poppies.*

The—the poppies in her hand are quite nice, of course, but the rest of it…. Why couldn't she have dressed it!

MACLEAN   This must stop! I shall talk to her tonight!

MRS. MACLEAN   Oh, it seems that no matter what one does, the wild blood will show itself!

MRS. REDFERN and CISSIE enter. MACLEAN hastily covers the statue, but the cloth falls on the floor as he hurries to greet them.

MRS. REDFERN   My dear Mr. Maclean—and Mrs. Maclean—how are you? Such a pleasure to see you again.

CISSIE   Dear Mrs. Maclean!

MRS. REDFERN   We were afraid, Cissie and I, that you would think us very neglectful—to let you be here so long—without coming to see you, but those dreadful rains, and my neuralgia you know—

MRS. MACLEAN   The idea! We are delighted—

MACLEAN   Our pleasure of pleasures, dear friend. Be seated, be seated.

> *Both he and MRS. MACLEAN are trying to get them seated with their backs to the statue.*

MRS. MACLEAN   Do sit here, Mrs. Redfern. And Cissie, let me put you in this chair, so comfortable. It was always Ida's favourite chair when she was here.

MRS. REDFERN   So Ida is married. I must congratulate you. Such a good match! And the Attorney-General has a private fortune, I understand? Is it so?

MRS. MACLEAN   Oh yes, my son-in-law is very well off indeed, and so prominent, politically!

MACLEAN   And a true Christian, Mrs. Redfern.

> *MARY enters with teapot.*

MRS. MACLEAN   Oh yes, indeed; we could never have given him our daughter had it been otherwise, as I'm sure you know, dear Mrs. Redfern!

MRS. REDFERN   Yes indeed. As I was saying, with Ida so happily married and Harold almost ready for the ministry, the dear boy, you are singularly blessed in your children. We have seen a great deal of Harry lately. Haven't we, Cissie!

> *MRS. MACLEAN pours tea. MARY distributes to all except CISSIE, who refuses it. MARY exits.*

CISSIE   Oh, Mama!

MRS. MACLEAN   He has written us so gratefully of your kindness, and Cissie's. I'm sure Cissie would be kind to Harry.

MACLEAN   We expect him tomorrow from his visit to my brother at Inleteah. Next month he goes to Victoria permanently to take up the work there.

CISSIE   Isn't it splendid! Such a large church!

MACLEAN   The Bishop himself is personally interested.

MRS. REDFERN   Mrs. Maclean, I hear you have brought Tom Conroy's daughter home with you. Is that really so?

MRS. MACLEAN   Yes. It seemed the only thing to do. Her education is finished of course. The friends she lived with have gone abroad. She pleaded so to come up for a visit that we consented. So, for the present, Precious is with us.

CISSIE   "Precious." What a queer name! Whoever called her that?

MRS. REDFERN   Cissie dear!

MACLEAN   The name is a translation. She was baptised "Hluut'ws"—an Indian name which means "Precious."

CISSIE   An Indian name!

MRS. REDFERN   Cissie! Do tell me, Mrs. Maclean, what sort of a girl is she now? Does she show any.... Cissie, perhaps you would like to walk in the garden a little, since you don't care for tea?

CISSIE   No, thank you, Mama. Why shouldn't you talk in front of me? Is she pretty, Mrs. Maclean? And is—are Harry and Ida fond of her?

MACLEAN   Neither Ida nor Harold have seen her since she was a little girl. We have had her educated in California.

CISSIE   I want to see her.

MRS. REDFERN   Your children of course are ignorant, er—

MRS. MACLEAN   Cissie, my dear, if you want to see Precious I suggest that you walk down to the end of the garden to meet her. It would be so nice for the two girls to meet in that way—so informal.

MRS. REDFERN   Yes! What a delightful idea! Do as Mrs. Maclean suggests, darling.

CISSIE   Dear Mrs. Maclean. You always think of such dear things.

CISSIE exits on veranda, and stops out of sight of the women, but within earshot.

MRS. REDFERN   I was saying, you really have kept your children ignorant...?

MRS. MACLEAN   Entirely ignorant of everything connected with Precious, except that Mr. Maclean and I have provided for this girl who is a very distant cousin of mine. The girl herself is ignorant of her Indian blood.

CISSIE   What! Indian blood!

MRS. REDFERN   Cissie! What are you doing there!

CISSIE   (*entering*) Indian blood! You never told me, Mama! How disgusting! I had no idea that her mother... was she an Indian?

MRS. MACLEAN   Oh dear!

MRS. REDFERN   Not quite. Only half... or even less. These are things you cannot possibly understand. You should not hear of them. Conroy's mother is an important relative of Mrs. Maclean's, she disinherited her son, who is now dead, for his connection— marriage—with the woman—er—when the child was born, I mean. No one knows anything about this poor girl's taint except ourselves and a few old residents, and the Indians of course. You must never allude to it. I suppose, Mrs. Maclean, in California they might not think so much about it, even if it were generally known. I've heard there are places where Indian blood and, er, these... connections, are not so condemned. Here, of course, it is such a terrible disgrace. Remember, Cissie, no nice young girl is supposed to know such things, much less speak of them.

MRS. MACLEAN   Yes, remember that, Cissie. Even Mary treats her with the greatest rudeness but Precious seems not to notice it particularly. Isn't it strange that the Indians have such a contempt for those with white blood, almost as we feel about Indian blood!

That is chiefly why Precious can't remain here with us, of course. Robert would lose his influence.

CISSIE   To think of your actually adopting her!

MRS. MACLEAN   That we felt to be our duty.

MRS. REDFERN   Conroy's mother sent the money, I believe. She is quite a wealthy woman. Harry has expectations from her…

MRS. MACLEAN   Great Aunt Eliza felt it so terribly! She appealed to us, and when she offered to set aside a sum yearly for Precious' education we felt that we had not the right to refuse. Though, of course, we could not bring her up in our own home with Ida and Harry growing up.

CISSIE   I should say not!

MACLEAN   We are all God's children, Cissie, red and white. He was the maker of us all—

MRS. MACLEAN   There are not many Christians like my husband! You know, Mrs. Redfern, Mr. Maclean has made himself very much disliked—feared at Ottawa lately.

MRS. REDFERN   It was something about Indian marriages, was it not? I don't think I quite understand. Cissie dear, go into the garden.

CISSIE   I don't see why! I never hear any news!

She exits, the women watching, making sure she does go this time.

MRS. MACLEAN   Tell Mrs. Redfern, dear—

MACLEAN   My mission to Ottawa, which I will not yet believe was fruitless, was to urge that some law be passed compelling all men, and I aimed principally at white men who have—er—taken up their abode with native women or the descendants of native women, to marry these women legally and through the church.

MRS. REDFERN   You are entirely right. Oh, the sin that we see about us every day! It has been so hard to keep it all from Cissie.

MRS. MACLEAN   These women… some of them almost as white as we are, only think of it, almost as white!

MRS. REDFERN   And what did the authorities at Ottawa say?

MRS. MACLEAN   Just fancy! One of them, I believe it was the Prime Minister himself, said he didn't think it could be enforced. So ridiculous! He said too if it could be enforced it would work great injustice on men. It would make them lose their honourable standing in the community, ruin their careers. Of course some quite brilliant men *have* had these—

MRS. REDFERN   Dear me!

MRS. MACLEAN   Oh, but Robert answered him! Tell Mrs. Redfern what you said to him, dear.

MRS. REDFERN   Oh I'm sure it was something splendid. Of course, I am very much interested, very much interested, about the Indians, you know. And of course I fully agree with you that they ought to be married, and so forth. But, my dear friends, my object in sending Cissie out of the room was to speak of quite another matter. It's about Harry.

MACLEAN   I trust that my son—

MRS. REDFERN   Oh no, no. Don't misunderstand me. I am sure Harry is blameless. Let me explain. Cissie is so sensitive and so very nervous—though I have her on a tonic now and I must say it is doing her good. However, as I was saying, she is very sensitive. She has one of those delicate flower-like natures which so easily becomes hysterical, especially when in love. Oh, I know! I was precisely the same myself when Mr. Redfern was courting me. One day I saw him walking down the village street with the Postmaster's daughter and it affected me so—you see he hadn't definitely proposed to me yet—that I simply went into one fit of hysterics after another. They had to put me to bed with a hot water bottle at my feet.

MRS. MACLEAN   Really!

MRS. REDFERN   You see, it was such a small town, and there really was no other young man whom I could have married, and it seemed.... It's moments like those that make a girl realise what a serious and sacred thing marriage is.

MRS. MACLEAN   Yes, indeed.

MRS. REDFERN   And really, my dear friends, something must be done. I do my best to encourage Cissie but the fact is Harry has not proved a very ardent lover!

MACLEAN   Perhaps you were too faithful a chaperone, ha, ha—

MRS. REDFERN   I trust I *am* a careful mother, Mr. Maclean. But, well—in this instance I simply threw discretion to the winds, and... he did not propose. He absolutely did not propose!

MACLEAN   I can believe that Harold felt it unnecessary, knowing that I had arranged everything. Still, it was an oversight.

MRS. REDFERN   An oversight which has played havoc with my darling's nerves! She has become obsessed with fear of some other girl. She feels terribly about your having brought Miss Conroy here. She says she has a premonition that Harry will fall in love with her.

MRS. MACLEAN   Oh, the dear child!

MRS. REDFERN   Oh, you mustn't think I attach much importance to Cissie's premonitions, because she has them about every girl Harry has ever met. But I feel I must ask you to do something definite when Harry arrives. Cissie can't stand another month of torture, expecting a proposal every minute, encouraging it by every delicate means that a young lady can use, and then not receiving it. She is so irritable now we can hardly live with her!

MACLEAN   I will notify Harry at the first convenient moment; and I can assure you, my dear, he will immediately offer himself to Cissie in the approved manner. Have no more worries about the matter.

MRS. REDFERN   Oh, I felt sure of your sympathy, or I would not have spoken so openly. Now tell me about your protegée before Cissie returns. This girl, does she show anything in her appearance at all, or in her nature?

MRS. MACLEAN   Oh Precious is—

> *PRECIOUS enters, not having heard any of the previous conversation.*

PRECIOUS   On the spot, Lallie, and pretty much dilapidated too. Look at me!

MRS. MACLEAN   Mercy! Precious! What *have* you been doing?

PRECIOUS   Doing? I've been done! Mauled by a grizzly and insulted by a woman and, upon my word, I think I prefer the grizzly!

MRS. MACLEAN   Explain yourself, child!

MRS. REDFERN   Dear me!

PRECIOUS   Give me time, Lallie dear. I've been running so, I'm out of breath. I was racing down toward the end of the garden and I nearly ran over a—

MRS. MACLEAN   A grizzly in the garden! Oh Robert!

PRECIOUS   No, no, Lallie. A snip of a girl, all befrilled in dotted swiss innocence, with an expression like a smug white cat that has just licked up all the cream and seen the puppy whipped for it—

They realise that it's CISSIE she's talking of.

MACLEAN   Precious. I think we had better—

MRS. MACLEAN   Precious, please!

PRECIOUS   I'm telling it as fast as I can, Lallie. She said "Well, run on, if you want to. Catch up with your *friend*." And the tone she used! The white cat. Whom do you suppose she meant? Louis Prince, the half-breed! Such insolence.

MACLEAN   But the grizzly, child. Where was the grizzly?

PRECIOUS   In the woods. May I have some tea, Lallie? (*MRS. MACLEAN gives her tea.*) I had gone as far up the mountain as I could climb—

MRS. MACLEAN   Oh, Precious! I have warned you—

PRECIOUS   I know, Lallie! But they call me, those great deep forests and those fierce old peaks and I must go.

MRS. MACLEAN   For goodness sake, Precious!

PRECIOUS   I had been lying on the moss under the pines for some time when I heard a shot. It occurred to me that I had better hit the trail for home if I didn't want some ambitious hunter to bag me, so I crawled out of the bush, and found the trail again—

Left to right: Bob Rathie (Maclean), Odessa Shuquaya (Precious),
Fran Burnside (Mrs. Redfern)
photo by Christopher LeMay

MRS. REDFERN   Well, I should call it very dangerous and
a foolhardy thing, to go off the trail into the jungle of
undergrowth so far from the village.

PRECIOUS   Oh, I have an instinct for the trail I have discovered.

MRS. MACLEAN   Nonsense, Precious! Don't say such an absurd
thing!

PRECIOUS   Lallie dear, you are always reproving me for
having instincts! As I was going down the steep trail I heard
something—a crashing in the brush. Then the pad-pad of
something on the ground behind me—

MRS. MACLEAN & MRS. REDFERN   Oh!

PRECIOUS   It was a grizzly and he was hurrying. He had been wounded, and was dropping blood as he ran. I made for the tree, and the grizzly made for me. I meant to put the tree between us and play tag around it if I could.

MRS. MACLEAN & MRS. REDFERN   Oh!

PRECIOUS   Just as I dashed behind the tree I saw a man running up the trail beneath me, and I screamed. The bear and I had our game of tag. He made a wide reach for me, in the third round I think it was, which was the grizzly's from the start. He got my skirt, and I thought it was all over, Lallie, when suddenly he turned with a roar. When I could grasp anything, I saw that he was having a fight to the finish with Louis Prince.

MACLEAN   The man was—

PRECIOUS   Yes, Louis Prince. He had leaped up like—like a wild cat. Oh, I wish you could have seen him. He had only his knife, and every time the bear rushed at him he sprang aside and lunged at him. Sometimes he got him and sometimes he missed. Once he slipped on the bloody moss.

MRS. MACLEAN   Oh. Was he killed?

PRECIOUS   Killed? He whirled up like a sudden wind. It was beautiful! And his grace, his daring! I wouldn't have missed it for anything in the world. Then in a moment Louis Prince saw his chance. He plunged his knife into the side of the grizzly's neck and that bear will bite no more!

MACLEAN   Thank God!

PRECIOUS   Then Louis Prince—and I assure you there wasn't a trace of expression on his face—Louis Prince wiped his knife on his sash and said "Pretty bad you walk in woods and no gun, Miss Conroy." I sat down suddenly.

MRS. MACLEAN   Oh, poor child, you fainted?

PRECIOUS   No, I didn't faint, Lallie, but my spine shut up like a clasp knife.

MRS. MACLEAN   Oh dear! Oh dear!

MRS. REDFERN   Dear me!

PRECIOUS   Louis Prince said "Not good stay here. Maybe more grizzly come." Then—now don't *you* feel faint, Lallie—then he swung me over his shoulder—

MRS. MACLEAN   Precious!

PRECIOUS   Swung me over his shoulder, Lallie, like a bale of furs and dropped down over the cliff with me. Would you think he had such muscles? The strength of him! Oh, it was mighty!

MRS. REDFERN   Really?

MRS. MACLEAN   My dear!

PRECIOUS   He wouldn't put me down. He stalked on as if he didn't even hear me until we were nearly in sight of the house when he sat me on my feet, still without a word, and strode down the hill ahead of me.

> *CISSIE enters from garden.*

CISSIE   Well, Mama, have you finished your gossip?

PRECIOUS   The white cat. Let me get out of this.

MRS. MACLEAN   Precious, this is Miss Redfern, and this is Mrs. Redfern. Dear Mrs. Redfern, I must apologise. In my excitement and anxiety I am afraid I forgot to introduce Precious. My adopted daughter, Precious Conroy.

MRS. REDFERN   Don't mention it, Mrs. Maclean. I think she has sufficiently introduced herself.

MRS. MACLEAN   Mrs. Redfern and her daughter are great friends of Harry's.

MRS. REDFERN   Oh, in the matter of being Harry's friend, I abdicate in Cissie's favour.

CISSIE   Oh, Mama!

PRECIOUS   Ah—Harry's friends? Poor Harry, he doesn't have much choice of friends up here in the wilds, does he!

MRS. MACLEAN   Precious! Harry had not always lived up here in the wilds, as you call it. He has seen enough of the world, at least to know what friends to choose.

PRECIOUS   Yes, Lallie dear, and that must make it all the harder, mustn't it?

> MARY *enters and gathers up tea things, but not PRECIOUS's cup.*

MACLEAN   Er—I have a few matters—in my study demanding attention—and if you will excuse me—

MRS. REDFERN   Oh certainly, don't let us keep you.

> *MACLEAN exits.*

You say you expect Harry tomorrow, Mrs. Maclean? How anxious you must be to see him again.

MRS. MACLEAN   Yes indeed, it is almost a year since I have had a real look at him.

PRECIOUS   Mary, here is my cup.

MARY   Huh! You bring him. (*MARY exits.*)

PRECIOUS   I wonder why Mary absolutely refuses to wait on me? I've decided that Indians are not polite. Courageous, but not polite.

CISSIE   The Indian is a child of nature, Miss... er... Conroy.

PRECIOUS   Oh, is he?

CISSIE   You seem to take to the Indian dress quite naturally.

PRECIOUS   It is picturesque. It rather fascinates me. I suppose partly because I've never seen anything like it before.

MRS. MACLEAN   Please! Precious, can't you and Cissie talk of something else besides Indians! What has come over you? You know what *I* think of that Indian skirt. She will wear it. It is what she calls "artistic."

PRECIOUS   I imagine we could talk of several things, Lallie. Miss Redfern has a wide range of topics, I don't doubt. We will discuss salmon canning presently, and the social advantages of Nass River.

MRS. MACLEAN   Precious!

PRECIOUS   And by the time we have exhausted that subject, Miss Redfern will be going home.

MRS. REDFERN   (*rising*) I am sure we can go now, if our welcome is outstayed!

MRS. MACLEAN   My dear Mrs. Redfern—the idea! When I am so delighted to have you! It is only Precious' carelessness. Precious dear, you know you are very brusque. It is no wonder that people misunderstand you.

> *MRS. REDFERN sits down again.*

PRECIOUS   Oh, do you think they do, Lallie? I should so hate to be misunderstood.

> *Pause. All, except PRECIOUS, are uncomfortable.*

Lallie, it has just struck me that although I have heard about little else but that wonderful son of yours since I came here, yet you have never shown me a photograph of him. I should think you'd have the walls plastered with them.

MRS. REDFERN   Dear me! What would our minister say to that?

MRS. MACLEAN   Mr. Maclean does not believe in human photographs. I mean photos of human beings. He considers it breaks the second commandment. You know it says "or any likeness of anything that is in heaven above or that is in the earth beneath." And of course a photograph is a likeness.

PRECIOUS   Sometimes!

MRS. REDFERN   I think that Harry is truly happy now in the idea of the ministry, Mrs. Maclean, don't you?

MRS. MACLEAN   We believe and trust so.

PRECIOUS   Wasn't Lallie's paragon son always happy in the idea of converting the heathen—red and white?

MRS. MACLEAN   My dear! Not at first. He didn't feel the "call." But of course he allowed his father to judge for him. It would have looked strange indeed to the world if the only son of so consecrated a man as Mr. Maclean should have chosen any other calling.

MRS. REDFERN   It must have relieved you so, at the time of his accident I mean, to feel that, if it had been fatal, at least he was prepared.

PRECIOUS   If you'll excuse me, I think I'll take my cup to the... child of nature, and mend my skirt.

CISSIE   I scolded Harry for bathing in water he knew nothing about. You know they always say that these Santa Cruz waters are dangerous.

MRS. REDFERN   Did he ever hear who was the brave girl who rescued him?

MRS. MACLEAN   No! He was never able to find out. Oh, we were so anxious when we had sent him to California for his cough.

MRS. REDFERN   You know she jumped in with all her clothes on—out of a boat you know.

>   *PRECIOUS drops cup with a smash.*

MRS. MACLEAN   Mercy, Precious! How careless of you! My new cups!

PRECIOUS   Was that Harry?

MRS. MACLEAN   What is the matter, child?

PRECIOUS   Harry.... Oh!

CISSIE   It was at Santa Cruz! A girl did it—a girl! What do *you* know about it? *(They lock eyes.)* You were the girl. It was you! Ugh!

PRECIOUS   Was that Harry? Are you sure?

CISSIE   Well, what if it was? What if it was, I say? What is it to you!

PRECIOUS   Don't dare say it if it isn't true.

CISSIE   Oh it was you. I can see it was. You'd do it—

PRECIOUS   Harry, who is coming tomorrow... ah!

CISSIE   He's coming to me, not to you! To me, do you hear!

MRS. REDFERN   Cissie!

CISSIE   Harry's mine! Mine! I know he is! Everybody says so. It's all understood.

MRS. REDFERN   Cissie, be calm.

CISSIE   Leave me alone, Mama! You know I had a premonition! (*to PRECIOUS*) It won't do you any good! He'd never marry you—you! Do you know what you are? A—

MRS. MACLEAN   Cissie. Be silent!

CISSIE   (*sobbing*) Mama, she can't have him!

MRS. MACLEAN   I will help you take Cissie home, Mrs. Redfern. Poor Precious is completely unstrung after her fright from the grizzly. I really must insist on your taking Cissie away!

MRS. REDFERN   It was not all Cissie's fault, Mrs. Maclean. She is so nervous naturally, poor child! And then the excitement of expecting Harry…

PRECIOUS   Take her away, Lallie. I can't bear her.

MRS. REDFERN   We are going as fast as possible, Miss Conroy. Come, darling. Come with Mama.

MRS. MACLEAN   Control yourself, Cissie dear. (*exits with MRS. REDFERN and CISSIE*)

PRECIOUS   (*sinking onto chair*) If he should come!

> *Time passes. PRECIOUS sinks into reverie. Enter LOUIS Prince, pauses, looking at her.*

LOUIS   Bisbis hl masaaa chx. (*speaking with the accent of an educated white English-speaking Canadian*) Light-bringer.

PRECIOUS   (*still in reverie*) Lallie…

> *LOUIS comes up behind PRECIOUS. Lightly touches her hair. PRECIOUS, thinking that MRS. MACLEAN is behind her, raises her arms to her. LOUIS raises her from behind. She turns in his grasp and gives a low cry.*

PRECIOUS   Lal—

LOUIS   (*puts hand over her mouth*) Don't scream! Why are you afraid?

PRECIOUS   Let me go. What are you doing here, Louis Prince?

LOUIS   (*relapsing into Indian dialect*) I come bring you table. You tink Louis Prince one grizzly?

PRECIOUS   The grizzly.... Yes, you—you saved my life. I will ask
Mr. Maclean to help you, to do something for you.

LOUIS   I no want. What for you feel bad to me?

PRECIOUS   No, I don't...

LOUIS   Yes. You feel bad here to me. (*puts hand on breast*) What
for? My father—Sim'oogit—Chief all injun. Mot'er she half-breed.
Louis Prince white man too—like you—and big injun. Strong
man—make table for you. Kill grizzly for you. Pack you on
shoulder like small white rabbit. Louis Prince strong man and
chief's son. Why you have the bad heart for him?

PRECIOUS   (*trying to edge away*) I... haven't the bad heart for you.
I know you are brave—

LOUIS   Then what for—bah! No good talk to woman! Listen. One
rich Injun Spallumcheen—he got daughter. Eyes like deer and
skin like berries. She say "Young men come. T'ey bring much skin
and blanket to my fat'er house and t'ey speak of me!" She say
"What for you come not wit skin and blanket to my fat'er house?"

PRECIOUS   (*recovering*) She has not the bad heart for you, Louis
Prince.

LOUIS   She have te heart on fire for me. What good! I not want
woman wit hair of seal and face like berries. She have te heart on
fire for me—but I have te heart on fire for woman wit te face like
white waters and te hair like red cloud. (*gently takes hold of her
hair*)

PRECIOUS   (*drawing back in alarm yet fascinated*) For me? How
dare you!

LOUIS   You make fire at my heart. You t'ink for noting you do
dat? You tink fire eat my heart slow... slow... for noting? No.
(*PRECIOUS tries to shake herself free from his grasp.*) You my
woman. Soon I take you.

PRECIOUS   You! How dare you touch me! I'd kill you. (*She
snatches up a bronze paperweight. After brief struggle he takes
it from her.*)

LOUIS   Good! You pretty good devil, too. (*tosses paperweight on
table*)

> *Sound of the church bell ringing.*

Bell ring. I go church now. *(exit)*

PRECIOUS   *(silent for a moment)* Insolent devil! …splendid! "Louis Prince strong man and Chief's son." So that was why he killed my grizzly…. The most human person I've found here yet. *(pause)* I shall not tell Lallie.

> *Enter MRS. MACLEAN.*

MRS. MACLEAN   You seem dreadfully upset, Precious. I am concerned about you.

PRECIOUS   *(embracing her)* Oh, Lallie!

MRS. MACLEAN   There, there, dear.

PRECIOUS   Oh Lallie, Lallie. I am going to love you so much!

MRS. MACLEAN   My dear child!

PRECIOUS   So much! You have given me everything. *(Pause. PRECIOUS walks to the french windows and looks out.)* Lallie—

MRS. MACLEAN   Yes, what?

PRECIOUS   I… was that the bell for service?

MRS. MACLEAN   Why of course. What did you think it was? It rings half an hour before church time so that the people can come in from the logging camps and the other village. I don't know if I told you, Precious, but we have to be *very* particular about it on account of the Anglican Missionary at the other village. He has actually invited some of our converts to attend his services. He was here for years before Robert came and he never fails to take advantage of the fact, and the priest up the river is just as bad.

PRECIOUS   Yes, you told me. *(pause)* Lallie—

MRS. MACLEAN   What is it, Precious!

PRECIOUS   Do you suppose it could have been—Harry?

MRS. MACLEAN   I suppose it is quite possible. And if so, I am sure it was a very brave thing to do. But I'm sorry you spoke of it in front of Cissie.

PRECIOUS   Why?

MRS. MACLEAN   Because, while Harry and Cissie are not exactly engaged, Harry knows his father's wishes. And Cissie herself—

PRECIOUS   She—seemed to be afraid I might interfere with her, didn't she!

MRS. MACLEAN   Such nonsense! As if... the idea!

PRECIOUS   Yes, but Lallie, suppose I should interfere? I know I am not so pretty, not in the same way...

MRS. MACLEAN   Precious! Not another word! I will not hear it!

PRECIOUS   Why Lallie?

MRS. MACLEAN   It is utterly impossible! Atrocious! Don't say such a thing again! Harry's marriage to Cissie is practically arranged. In fact, Mr. Maclean expects to solemnise their union before Harry goes to Victoria... perhaps next month.

PRECIOUS   *(masking)* I was just talking, Lallie. She is welcome to him. It is not—really—all that likely—that he... *is* the man... I pulled out of the water, is it? So many people get upturned and rescued, you know. Someone always goes in after them. And even if it should be Harry, it wouldn't make any difference to her, or him. How could it!

MRS. MACLEAN   No, of course not.

PRECIOUS   If you will excuse me, Lallie. I will go and rest a few moments.

MRS. MACLEAN   You will be ready in time for service, Precious?

PRECIOUS   Not today, Lallie. I can't worship with Father's congregation this afternoon.

MRS. MACLEAN   Oh!

PRECIOUS   There dear, don't be shocked. I can't feel as you do about them. The Indians appeal to me—because they are of the woods. They belong... Lallie, did you ever feel that the woods were calling, calling and that you must go? If I stayed here, some night I should run away, some night when the moon was throwing back shadows on the grim face of the forest, and those great pines were beckoning. I should plunge into their midst and never be seen again.

MRS. MACLEAN   It is absurd and—unladylike—for you to talk in that way. I must request you not to do it—*especially in front of people.*

PRECIOUS   But Lallie dear, if I feel like that—

MRS. MACLEAN   I think you'll see what I mean, Precious, when I tell you that Louis Prince said just the same thing when he came back from college.

PRECIOUS   College! Louis Prince! Why he can hardly speak English! How long since he came back?

MRS. MACLEAN   Three years, my dear. You mustn't be surprised. It always happens so. Indians are like that. Degradation is natural to them, though sometimes I believe Louis talks in that Indian way just to annoy us.

PRECIOUS   But Lallie, you can't call it degradation for an Indian to be an Indian. You don't blame a pine tree because it doesn't grow mignonettes. Oh—was it Prince I heard play the violin last night? Was it?

MRS. MACLEAN   Yes, he's the only person here who has one. He once played very brilliantly they say. He even gave a special concert for the Governor General at Rideau Hall. They said he had quite a talent for composing. He goes off into the woods now sometimes and makes up the weirdest things—

PRECIOUS   You know last night—when I was looking out of my window at the forest so deep and strange and dark—I heard that violin away in the pines, wailing with the wind—well—perhaps you've heard it—but it was Rodolfo's song from *La Bohème*.

"Chi son? Sono un poeta.
Che cosa faccio? Scrivo.
E come vivo? Vivo."

To hear that, up here, that one voice only out of the immense dark silence, it was the most wonderful thing I've ever heard— and the most terrible.

MRS. MACLEAN   I'm sure it's something Robert would not like to hear at all.

PRECIOUS   Then it went off into another theme—terrible—mighty, as if the forest and the mountains had suddenly become vocal. If

Father could have heard that—I mean if he could understand it—he'd pull up the mission house and depart.

MRS. MACLEAN   Precious! What a wicked thing to say! Nothing could make Robert desert his post. Nothing!

MACLEAN   (*entering*) Martha, we will start the service in a few moments. The roof of the mission house is unsafe from all the rain, and I have told Louis Prince to assemble our people in my study. Precious, I want to talk to you.

MRS. MACLEAN   I'll tell Mary to bring chairs. (*exits, calling to MARY*)

MACLEAN   Precious, you were brought very near to death today. Did you feel that you were prepared?

PRECIOUS   I don't know, Father. I don't think that I felt anything about it. You haven't much time for serious reflection when a grizzly is coming for you, you know.

MACLEAN   Do you feel now that you are prepared?

PRECIOUS   I can't feel that I ought to worry about dying! When there is such splendid life to be lived!

MACLEAN   That is a terrible thing to hear from the lips of a child of my house. But I will speak to you more of that later. It is of your—your work as you call it—that I want to speak to you now. Your thoughts are all of this... this making of statues. It is not right.

PRECIOUS   Father, I can't see that sculpture is a religious question at all! I am sorry but—

MACLEAN   What of the moral question then?

PRECIOUS   Father, one cannot speak of art in that way. Art is not limited that way. It is older than churches. It was the inspiration of people who never knew what you call morality.

MACLEAN   Neither religious nor moral. Then what is this art?

PRECIOUS   Oh, it's the beauty of life! Beauty that colours the sea and the forest and gives us dreams and makes us love.

MACLEAN   I do not understand such words. To me they mean nothing. I ask you this. How can you—a virtuous woman—stand

in the light of day and carve forms of unclothed humanity?
(*points to statue*)

PRECIOUS   Who uncovered it?

MACLEAN   I did!

PRECIOUS   You had no right—

MACLEAN   No right—I, no right! I am the master of this house
and God's minister—the appointed caretaker of souls!

PRECIOUS   No! You have no right over my soul. It is my own
affair.

> *LOUIS Prince passes along outside, ringing a large bell.*

MACLEAN   You speak blasphemy. It is now time for the service.
I will talk to you again later. But you must realise this—that
only a woman dead to all sense of decency could spend hours in
creation and contemplation of the naked form. Crush out this art,
child. Crush it out, and pray. (*exit*)

> *Sounds of praying off. LOUIS returns and stands in doorway
> watching PRECIOUS.*

PRECIOUS   Crush it out! Oh, I can't bear it! It is all so unreal.
Listen to that! There is only one real thing in the world, my
poppy woman—only one real thing. And they have missed it!
Tomorrow... tomorrow!

> *"Shall We Gather At the River" by Robert Lowry sung in
> English by the congregation begins off.*

Act II

Late afternoon, near sunset.

Koksilah sits on the ground with her baby. SIM'OOGIT is readying some fishing gear. LOUIS Prince is sitting on the church steps, playing his violin. He finishes as CONROY enters, quite drunk.

CONROY   Mr. Maclean inside?

LOUIS   No, he go up river las' night.

CONROY   Mrs. Maclean?

LOUIS   She up house. (*CONROY exits. LOUIS speaks with a distinct change of accent.*) Father, are you going fishing this evening?

SIM'OOGIT   Yes. But first, I want to speak to you. Don't call me Father, Hlaagoo't. You've forgotten that you're my son and instead (*pointing to church*) you serve that old white man who speaks so foolishly.

LOUIS   Yet—he makes the medicine of his people.

SIM'OOGIT   His medicine is foolish. I've only been once inside that house, that evil looking house, he's set up among the totems of my people. In a very loud voice he told of a great spirit which is his slave and which will burn us all with a never-ending fire.

LOUIS   White men say this fire is a strong medicine. I don't know.

SIM'OOGIT   But then Halyte, whose medicine is strong, took a white-hot stone from the stove and held it in his hand without burning. And Halyte said "If your God is so strong, then *you* hold this hot stone in your hand without burning." But the old man couldn't. So I'm not afraid of this Spirit of his. Only it makes men foolish and fond of much talking. Don't go to this white man's house again.

LOUIS   Father, I know all the white man's medicine. I learned it when I lived in the east, where there are as many totems of his tribe as there are trees in the forest, and as many people as there are salmon in the mouth of the river.

SIM'OOGIT   Yes. Yes. This is why I sent you to the great white village, that you will be the mightiest of all chiefs when I'm gone, having both the white and Indian medicines. And so by great cunning you will be able to drive the white tribe out of our land.

LOUIS   It is your dream.

SIM'OOGIT   No. Shall it not be so? Then for what have I spent my blankets and my furs and the substance of my tribe?

LOUIS   For a dream.

SIM'OOGIT   Was it for a dream that I didn't see your face through those long and evil years?

LOUIS   For a dream, Father, for a dream—

SIM'OOGIT   No—it is this white man's music. (*pointing to violin*) It is a devil and has put a spell on your spirit. It is a magic the white medicine men have worked that you shall not be a chief and save our people.

LOUIS   Yes, it is a magic both evil and good, for in it my heart dies and lives again. It is a voice speaking things from far away.

SIM'OOGIT   What does the voice say, Hlaagoo't? I can tell you if it is a lie or not.

LOUIS   Let me tell you a story.... Long ago there was a mighty man named Kalista. His father said "He will be a great chief after me and sit on the hills of council." But Kalista heard a voice speaking from afar. "I will be a mighty hunter in a country of my own." And one day in the forest he met a white deer and his heart burned, for she called to him "I am Yagoot!" and he knew it was love, and followed, and after many moons he caught Yagoot in a far strange country, and there he became indeed Kalista the Mighty Hunter in a country of his own. And Yagoot, the swift and white, was his. And he found that the dream was true because he obeyed the voice that called and Kalista lives forever in his mountain with Yagoot.

SIM'OOGIT   It is well that there are no white deer in this land.

LOUIS   I have heard a voice from far away, too. It says to me "Hlaagoo't, when you were with the white men and learned their medicine, you saw that they were not your people. You were a stranger among a strange tribe and your heart was bitter. Then

you came back here. But here they also now do not know you.
And again you are a stranger among a strange people, and your
heart is bitter."

SIM'OOGIT   No, son, this is magic. I will find a medicine to cure it.
You shall be a great chief. I have said it. I will give all my wealth,
if it has to be, to cure this magic. But you must not go to the
white man's house any more.

LOUIS   Father, you cannot cure this magic, or make me a place
among the people. That also is one of your dreams.

SIM'OOGIT   I did wrong when I mated with the white blood of
your mother, for now I have a son whose spirit is like that of
a weasel and whose heart is foolish.

MRS. MACLEAN and PRECIOUS enter.

MRS. MACLEAN   Good afternoon, Sim'oogit.

SIM'OOGIT   *(not looking at her)* Humph.

MRS. MACLEAN   Louis Prince, tell your father we wish him to
come to church.

LOUIS   *Gala nax_ nitswin ahl algax_hl naks'y gohl wilp ama
dalxasxw.*

SIM'OOGIT   *Hen ahl amstwaa Sim'oogit wa'y needi'n didalk_ lok'm
x_ aak_.* [1] *(exits)*

MRS. MACLEAN   What did he say, Louis?

LOUIS   *(not looking at her)* Oh, he say—he no time talk now.

PRECIOUS   It sounded longer than that and more positive!

MRS. MACLEAN   He probably said something rude. Indians can be
very insulting.

PRECIOUS   I suppose he thinks you insulting for coming here and
sticking your church among his family trees.

LOUIS stands back, looking at PRECIOUS.

MRS. MACLEAN   I dare say. He's not in the least grateful.

---

[1] For translation of Gitxsan, see page 70

PRECIOUS   Why did you build your church at the end of the village? Did you think you were setting a divine barrier between your converts and their native woods?

MRS. MACLEAN   What ideas you have, child!

PRECIOUS   A solid wall of churches couldn't keep me out of that wood. It's my favourite walk, or plunge I should say. So deep and cool. To go into it is more like taking a plunge into the sea... into the sea...

MRS. MACLEAN   What are you talking about, Precious?

PRECIOUS   Why wouldn't the old Indian talk to you? Oh Lallie! Look at the baby! Oh, the funny fat brown little thing! (PRECIOUS squats down beside Koksilah.) What a solemn little owl you are, baby. Not a smile. (to Koksilah with measuring gesture) Big baby!

> Koksilah smiles a proud friendly open smile—then looks to where SIM'OOGIT exited and her smile fades. She looks stoically in front of her as before. Pause.

Lallie, do you believe in reincarnation?

MRS. MACLEAN   What?!

PRECIOUS   No, of course you don't. But I am beginning to believe in it.

MRS. MACLEAN   Oh dear. Precious!

PRECIOUS   Now listen, Lallie. I was only a baby when my mother died and of course I can't remember her at all. But lately, since I've come here, I seem to remember her.

MRS. MACLEAN   Impossible!

PRECIOUS   And she is like that mother there, Lallie. It is a brown face that leans over me. Isn't that odd? So you see, I must have been an Indian baby in some former life.

MRS. MACLEAN   You worry me and distress me very much by saying such things, Precious. I wish you wouldn't do it. And do sit properly, if you must sit on the ground. You're squatting like a.... There, do get up from the ground. It's... it's damp.

PRECIOUS   (unheeding) Nox.

MRS. MACLEAN   What?

PRECIOUS   *Nox*—that is an Indian word, isn't it?

MRS. MACLEAN   Yes, it means "mother." Where did you hear it?

PRECIOUS   I don't know. That's the strange thing. It just comes to me. And all this, it's not new. It's old. Sometime, long ago, I have been here with my brown-faced mother, and I called her *Nox*.

MRS. MACLEAN   Nonsense! You've never been here before. Your mother was an English woman. I forbid you to say such things. You've heard the word here lately, of course. You are... so... visionary. *(entering church)* Are you coming to help me? *(exits)*

LOUIS   *(coming to PRECIOUS)* You sit on ground. Good!

PRECIOUS   You think I look good on the ground? Many thanks.

LOUIS   Not laugh! You sit like Injun woman, good!

PRECIOUS   Louis Prince. Why do you talk like Mary? You've been to school.

LOUIS   Who told you that. I talk like Injun.

PRECIOUS   Well, why do you? You know better. I don't think you ought to forget all you learned from the white man.

LOUIS   *(in correct English)* I only learned one thing from white men. I learned that I am an Indian. Sooner or later you learn. Then you forget everything else they teach you. *(reverting to "injun")* What good!

PRECIOUS   Why won't your father speak to Mrs. Maclean or me?

LOUIS   Injuns not talk to womans. Not good.

PRECIOUS   You too—when Mrs. Maclean speaks to you and you answer her—you always turn your head away. Is it against Indian law for men to look at women?

LOUIS   Yes. Injun look not at women. *(Pause. He looks at her very directly till she lifts her eyes to look at him.)* When Injun look at woman t'at mean t'at *his* woman he looks at. It is our legend. Every man has seen but one woman... his woman.

> They continue to look at each other. She breaks and turns towards church. He intercepts her.

Left to right: Jason Krowe (Louis), Odessa Shuquaya (Precious)
photo by Christopher LeMay

I skin grizzly for you.

PRECIOUS   Thank you, Louis Prince. Is that the knife you killed
him with. Yes? Sell it to me. How much?

LOUIS   Who you want to kill?

PRECIOUS   You, maybe.

LOUIS   Good, I give him.

> *He hands her the knife, blade foremost. In order to take it*
> *she reaches up to the hilt.*

PRECIOUS   What do you want for it, Louis Prince?

He grips her fingers over the hilt.

LOUIS   You maybe. *(She struggles to break free.)* By 'n' by, me I take you.

He releases her and she sticks the knife in her belt.

PRECIOUS   You say that to me once more, Louis Prince, and I'll run this through you. I'm not afraid of you—not any longer.

LOUIS   Good! I say it no more. *(exits as MRS. MACLEAN opens church door)*

MRS. MACLEAN   Do come in, Precious. *(PRECIOUS goes into the church. CONROY enters.)*

CONROY   Martha!

MRS. MACLEAN   Tom Conroy!

CONROY   Do you know me, Martha?

MRS. MACLEAN   Tom Conroy—I thought you were dead!

CONROY   Did you Martha? Fancy that.

MRS. MACLEAN   We had a telegram from your partner last year saying you had died at Sitka.

CONROY   Did you Martha? Fancy that.

MRS. MACLEAN   He said you had died and he wanted money to bury you, and we wired the bank to pay it.

CONROY   Did you Martha? Fancy... I almost died, Martha.

MRS. MACLEAN   You swindled us, you mean... you—

CONROY   I'm a poor unregenerate man, Cousin Martha. I was afraid to die. I couldn't face the judgement. No, I said, I'll get well. I'll work my fingers to the bone and I'll earn that burial money and I'll take it and I'll lay it at Cousin Martha's feet and I'll say "Martha, your prayers are answered. Look up Martha, the Lord has spared my life."

MRS. MACLEAN   Well—have you brought it?

CONROY   I didn't wait to get it, Martha. I'm going to send it. I couldn't wait to bring it for, I said, I must see Cousin Martha, the best friend a man ever had, patient and loving and generous.

It's your generosity I admire so, and I always remember it, Martha. I said, "I must be the first to greet her. Shall I wait to gather up a few paltry dollars when Cousin Martha is grievin' and thinkin' me dead? "No," I said, "I'll go to her. I'll go." What's the news of Mother? My sainted lady mother?

MRS. MACLEAN   How did you get here today? There's no boat.

CONROY   I'm living here now. I've been here a month. I've been fishin'. Oh, it's a hard life, in with Indians and Chinamen and the dead fish and the poor pay that a man can't live on. Here I am sick and hungry and with never a dollar to bless me—

MRS. MACLEAN   You find dollars for whiskey, just as you always did, I notice.

CONROY   It's the smell of the fish. It ruins your clothes. It makes you sick—you know my delicate stomach, Martha. Just a drop of whiskey. Oh, a teaspoonful, it keeps away the infection. Oh the poor fellows, good God-fearing men, I've seen die because there wasn't a drop of whiskey to save them, and no-one to say a prayer. Poor fellows, poor fellows.... What's your news of Mother? My sainted mother?

PRECIOUS   (*opening door and putting her head out*) Lallie, do you want—Oh, I beg your pardon. (*goes back in*)

CONROY   I seem to recognise that voice, Martha.

MRS. MACLEAN   Impossible, you can't. You must go at once. If—

CONROY   I knew it. I knew it. It's my little daughter, my only child. Take me to her, Martha.

MRS. MACLEAN   Tom Conroy, who told you that your daughter was here?

CONROY   Ah, you can't deceive a father's heart, Martha. You can't deceive a father's heart. I've heard her sweet little voice calling me too long to mistake it now.

MRS. MACLEAN   Stuff and nonsense. You gave her up only too gladly. And you've never once asked about her since.

CONROY   How could I? I wasn't fit. I was an unregenerate man, Martha. But now that she's grown such a fine strong girl and able to care for her own father—and him one o' life's poor wrecks.

I passed your holy husband on the beach a day or two ago and he didn't know me. Oh, these sufferin' years, how they've changed me!

MRS. MACLEAN   She thinks you are dead.

CONROY   Poor child, poor child. Let us go to her at once and tell her to rejoice with us. Let us go together, Martha. But first, there's one thing I'll ask you, as I have a right for I'm a white man, and a father. Have you put virtue into her? Can I receive her? Can I give her a father's blessin'? Or is there just cause and impediment?

MRS. MACLEAN   So that is what you came here for! I thought it was money.

CONROY   Money! What can money do, for a father? Money! It's the curse of the world, I say. I don't envy you your money, Martha, for all you're so generous and open-handed. No. Give me my child, my pretty child. That's all I ask.

MRS. MACLEAN   Do you want her to live as you live? You're insane.

CONROY   Insane! Because I love my child? Oh, the injustice. Of course I can't give her the comforts she's been accustomed to. But I don't envy you your money, Martha. I wouldn't take a dollar of it, not one dollar…. I couldn't be induced to take a dollar. Though some might say "Who has a better right to that money than Thomas Conroy?" My lady mother's money that you got taken from me! All on account of a squaw's brat!

PRECIOUS   (*putting head out*) Lallie, do come here a minute—oh! (*catching sight of CONROY*)

MRS. MACLEAN   (*moving CONROY away from door*) We did our duty in telling Great Aunt Eliza what she had a right to know. (*draws purse out*) I'll give you two dollars to go away now—quick.

CONROY   It's beneath you, Martha. It's beneath you.

PRECIOUS   (*stepping out*) I don't know what you want done in there, Lallie. (*tries to fasten door*)

MRS. MACLEAN   Five dollars then. It's all I have in my purse. You don't want to ruin your child's life.

CONROY   I wouldn't do it, Martha. You don't know what it is to have a father's heart. That's something you don't know. I'll see you again, Martha. And my pretty child. Have you put virtue into her? But I needn't ask. *(takes money)* The Lord reward you. *(MRS. MACLEAN goes up to PRECIOUS.)* That dime's worn too smooth, Martha. It won't pass. I'd rather go out of her life forever than... I'll see you again, Martha. *(exits mumbling)*

PRECIOUS   Who's your inebriate friend, Lallie?

MRS. MACLEAN   Come in, dear, quickly. *(goes into church, from inside)* Come Precious.

> *HARRY enters. PRECIOUS turns and meets his eyes.*

HARRY   You!

PRECIOUS   I knew that you would come to me!

> *MRS. MACLEAN comes out from church door.*

MRS. MACLEAN   Harry! Harry!

HARRY   Mother—Mother dear, how good to see you again. Where is Father?

MRS. MACLEAN   He had a sick call last night, dear, up the river. He can hardly return before morning. Oh, my precious boy! What a joy it is to have you with us again. But I am forgetting Precious.

HARRY   Precious?

MRS. MACLEAN   Our... daughter. This is Precious.

HARRY   Are you my adopted sister? Oh, but that is no relation at all.

MRS. MACLEAN   Not a very close one, dear.

HARRY   No, of course not. To think that it was you who saved me!

MRS. MACLEAN   What are you saying?

HARRY   Mother, it was Precious who saved me from drowning.

MRS. MACLEAN   Are you sure? Precious?

PRECIOUS   Yes. It is all true.

MRS. MACLEAN   My dear, brave girl! Why how you tremble, child!

PRECIOUS   Don't Lallie. It's nothing.

>   *Enter MACLEAN.*

MRS. MACLEAN   Here's your father!

HARRY   Father!

MACLEAN   Oh son, God has brought you back to us in safety.

HARRY   Yes, Father.

MRS. MACLEAN   Robert, you must have travelled all night. You cannot have rested at all!

MACLEAN   I shall rest now that I have seen my son again.

HARRY   Father, it was too much to do for me.

MRS. MACLEAN   Now I shall insist on taking you two dear men right home. You must be starving. Precious, will you finish arranging the prayer books for me? Then come home, dear. Come, Harry!

HARRY   Aren't you coming, Precious?

PRECIOUS   I am not hungry.

HARRY   But I want to see... to talk to you, to look at you across the table.

PRECIOUS   Talk to me here.

MRS. MACLEAN   Harry.

>   *Exit MACLEAN and MRS. MACLEAN.*

HARRY   I'll be back. *(exits)*

>   *PRECIOUS looks after him. LOUIS Prince enters, looks at PRECIOUS who doesn't see him. PRECIOUS goes after HARRY and watches him as LOUIS Prince continues to watch her until she turns and crosses to the church steps with her hand on the church door.*

LOUIS   Bisbis hl masaaa chx.

PRECIOUS   What is it, Louis Prince? Why do you call me?

LOUIS   When you come upon my path and would pass me, I see only that light has fallen across my dusk. I call to you "Bisbis hl masaaa chx." My dawn.

PRECIOUS   You have many names for me.

LOUIS   Dawn and Red Cloud, they are same in our language. Dawn of our race was in a cloud. Now we go—like shadows.

PRECIOUS   Oh, no. Your people—and you—will always pass silently back and forth through this forest—like trees moving—or spirits.

LOUIS   We have buried our dead in these trees since the morning of the world. Through all the years that cannot be counted, our people have lived in these forests—miles and miles from the North and back to the mountain and beyond the canyon far, far, to a land no white man knows. When the Father of Light has called us on, then hands of those who have most loved us have lifted us up and returned us to the arms of the forest. Among these pines our spirits have gone forth—and upward to the sun.

PRECIOUS   You speak as though you yourself had lived and died and lived again repeatedly in this wood!

> *The wind is heard now and then, sighing through the trees.*

LOUIS   Who knows? My mother was named The Wind-Promise because when she was born, fall winds were blowing pine-seeds over the earth. When she made my little cradle of cedar strands and wrapped me in it, she hung it in branches of this tree to rock in the wind, while she sat beneath weaving my father's cedar blanket and singing to me. When she died she passed among these branches. When my five brothers, full-grown men as I am, passed in the long cold spring, my father and I carried them up and left them, in high branches of this pine. Shall I say that I am living but they are dead? Do I not hear them speak in the moving of branches? Chiefs of the past—they are not dead. They sleep— even as I slept there (*points into trees*) as a little child when Wind-Promise sang, and all the mothers of our race whispered about my cradle.

PRECIOUS   Do you hear them now?

LOUIS   Always. Voices of my kindred. (*points to trees*) They do not
know death. Death is the white man's dream. It comes. It puts its
white hand on freedom to make it cease. A little hour is struggle
and dark, but freedom cannot cease. It calls—on—on—with
many voices.

PRECIOUS   With many voices?

LOUIS   The white hand must lose its hold. Their voice is law.
I know. I was in Montreal, in Ottawa—I played. First, white man's
music. It is music; but it was not for me. I played it only with my
fingers. But they said I had a great success—because the
Governor General and many important white men and women
clapped their white hands and said "Is this not a clever Indian
we have brought from the woods to amuse us?" Then *my* music
came. And they said "In a white man this would be genius. It
is too bad he's only an Indian." And they still clapped white
hands—with menace.

PRECIOUS   They did not understand?

LOUIS   No—and that was fine. They are men of flesh. White men
and sons of white men. I am not a man of flesh. I am of the earth.
My roots are deep in this earth.

PRECIOUS   Ah! (*She is now close to LOUIS Prince, looking at
the trees and the far mountain bathed in red sunset. PRECIOUS is
increasingly being entranced, awestruck.*)

LOUIS   I came back to my kindred. *They* received me. (*He means
the forest and mountains, not people.*) The white hand is upon this
village. It is a dark hour for my people. I have no place among
men. I left my father's house one morning very early. I went up
river in my canoe to the place where the waters fork and the great
canyon circles the mountains to the North. Great currents caught
at my canoe.

PRECIOUS   Ah!

LOUIS   It was death that I sought... that not even one splinter
of my canoe should be left to tell how I cast off the white hand.
The waters tossed me as a leaf, but never flung me on the rocks.
Rapids bore me on. And I saw that these also were my kindred
and could not harm me. So I stood to my paddle and guided my
way and came through the great canyon safely, which no man has

done in the memory of our people. There I left my canoe and
went across mountains into a new country of many lakes and
little streams and moss-covered rocks and pines, and deer.
I stayed there with my kindred for many weeks.

PRECIOUS   Why did you come back here?

LOUIS   Because they said to me "Where is the Woman?"

PRECIOUS   The woman—

LOUIS   There was none. Everything else living was joyous in
mating because it was Springtime, but not I. Earth lay like a great
woman in her arms of the sea, and the red clouds of the morning
were in her hair. (*He touches her hair and brings her into a loose
embrace. She seems unconscious of it.*) And the forest sang me
a mating song. Listen! (*They listen to the sound in the trees.*)

The air is a wind of love
From the wings of eagles mating;
O eagles, my sky is dark with your wings!
The hills and the waters pity me,
The pine trees reproach me,
The little moss whispers under my feet—
"Son of Earth, Brother,
Why comest thou hither alone?"
Oh! the wolf has his mate on the mountain—
Say, where is she, the Bearer of Morning,
My Bringer of Song?
Love in me waits to be born;
Where is she, the woman?

> *Wind. PRECIOUS is absorbed in the mystery of the theme;
> she hardly hears his words.*

PRECIOUS   (*murmuring*) The air is a wind of love
From the wings of eagles mating.
Eagles, my sky is dark with your wings.

LOUIS   I came back seeking the woman. It was a dark night when
I came back out of the forest. You stood at your window, holding
your candle high. Light shone upon your hair. All the world was
dark, but you stood there like young Morning, bright with the
sea-winds and strong with light. And my heart knew you. My
search was over. Bisbis hl masaaa chx; you... you are the woman.

HARRY   (*calling from off*) Precious.

> *LOUIS exits quickly into the forest behind the church as HARRY enters. PRECIOUS is unaware of all this, being caught up in the mystery.*

PRECIOUS   Love in me waits to be born.

HARRY   They sent me to fetch you.

PRECIOUS   Did *they* send you?

HARRY   This time I found you.

PRECIOUS   This time?

HARRY   Yes. Of course I searched for you.... Don't you know you're the only woman in the world for me.

PRECIOUS   The only woman? Did *you* seek me?

HARRY   I hunted Santa Cruz from end to end for two whole days and couldn't learn even your name.

PRECIOUS   And I had to leave that same night—without—knowing—

HARRY   You didn't care to know as I did.

PRECIOUS   You cared? Don't play with me. Don't say you cared if you didn't. Don't say it.

HARRY   (*kneeling by her*) I did care. I do. I've never forgotten you for a moment. Oh to think that we were brought ashore before we had thought about telling each other our names. How could we have let ourselves be separated so... casually?

PRECIOUS   Oh if I had known whether you really cared or not—it was that made it so hard to come away. I didn't mind not knowing your name. It didn't seem to matter. I felt that if you cared... you couldn't help just coming to me someday... and...

HARRY   And here I am.

PRECIOUS   Yes... here you are.

HARRY   (*taking her hand*) Your hands are like white wings. I want to feel them again—just like this I felt them pushing back my hair.

PRECIOUS   It was wet.

HARRY   Your arms held me.

PRECIOUS   Your head was on my breast and your hair—it was against my neck.

HARRY   Then I opened my eyes... and looked at *you!*

PRECIOUS   *You looked at me.*

HARRY   Your mouth was just above mine. (*He kisses her.*)

PRECIOUS   Oh, I have dreamed of this. I have lived in the hope of it. Sleeping, waking. I have seen your eyes as they opened that day close to mine. I have seen your face here (*puts hand on her breast*) and...

HARRY   What? What? Tell me more!

PRECIOUS   Isn't it enough that I have loved you like this... like this... day by day, hour by hour? You—you—only you. There has been nothing but you in the world. Isn't that enough?

HARRY   No. Kiss me! (*PRECIOUS holds back and looks at him.*) Kiss me. (*He holds her and kisses her.*) I love you. Your lips are like fire. (*Again he kisses her.*)

PRECIOUS   I love you. (*She rises.*) How soft and dark it grows.

HARRY   Must I take you in? (*His arm is around her.*)

PRECIOUS   Don't take me into the house. I want only you and the wind and the forest.

HARRY   I would go with you into the depths of the sea.

PRECIOUS   Not the sea tonight, Harry. Only the woods, the trees and warm sweet earth, and the wind above us, from the wind of eagles.

> *They kiss. He leads her off.*

Act III

> *Same as Act I, The next morning—full sunlight. PRECIOUS is modelling the clay figure on the turntable. HARRY stands close watching her. He picks up LOUIS Prince's knife, which lies on the stand with her tools and toys with it.*

HARRY   How wonderfully you do it! It's beautiful!

PRECIOUS   Do you like it? Be careful with that knife, Harry. It is sharp. Give it to me.

> *She takes the knife. Cuts a lump of clay, then sticks the knife in the pouch-bag at her belt.*

HARRY   I love to watch your hands. Perhaps it is because I knew them first. They are not hands to me. They are an expression of you. (*He kisses one of them.*)

PRECIOUS   An expression of me? Why that is beautiful, Harry. You should have been a poet, growing up here with them, and the earth calling "Give me an artist from among you! There are preachers enough!"

HARRY   (*looking toward door*) Ssh! It is odd you should say that because, please don't laugh at me, because I've always wanted to be a poet. Yes, really, and I've written verses, too.

PRECIOUS   Oh, show them to me...

HARRY   I haven't any of them now. You see... they were love poems.

PRECIOUS   Love poems—yes. Who did you write them to?

HARRY   Oh, not to anyone.

PRECIOUS   What happened to them?

HARRY   Father burned them all. He said they were the work of the devil. Then Mother cried so, that I promised I'd never write any more, and so I never have.

PRECIOUS   That doesn't seem possible!

HARRY   Perhaps it wouldn't be with a great genius. But I wasn't that. Yet it seems as if even a minor poet might have a right to follow his desire.

PRECIOUS   Every right in the world.

HARRY   Father didn't think that. So… I gave up writing. He took all the joy out of it for me. And when he killed the joy in it, the desire died too.

PRECIOUS   It shouldn't.

HARRY   No, I suppose not. But it's like that with me. It may be just because he is my father that he has been able to make me take his way all my life. I don't know. But some people have that power, Precious…. All you once thought beautiful they can make hideous and awful to you.

PRECIOUS   Oh, that is so wrong! You shouldn't give in.

HARRY   That is why he has always been able to make me give up whatever he doesn't like. Because when he talks about it in that way, I start to hate it.

PRECIOUS   It's wrong! Father feels like that about my modelling but I don't intend to stop it. I *can't*. It's part of *me*.

HARRY   I never met anyone like you, Precious! Everything about you is so strange; and yet, somehow, it seems so natural too. If I'd known you long ago—you would have made me think just as you do about things. You sweep me off my feet. Give me that hand again. *(takes her hand)* Clever hands—tender and soft—yet strong as a man's. *(kisses her hands)* What made them take to playing with clay, h'm?

PRECIOUS   I don't know. It appealed to me. And this morning, it means more to me than ever.

HARRY   Why?

PRECIOUS   Because of you, because of our love. I see now that the artist's creative desire is the same as Earth's—the desire to express love. I understand that now, since last night. I came here loving you; although I didn't know who "you" were. I only knew that the sea had cast up love into my arms.

HARRY   How beautiful you are!

PRECIOUS   The night before that day—

HARRY   Oh, wasn't it glorious. One of those magical white Californian nights simply drenched with moonlight.

PRECIOUS   You were up watching it too?

HARRY   Yes. One of the fellows I knew there had an automobile— owned it himself. We rode about in it all over town till the last café closed up. (*unconsciously lowers his voice and glances at door as if fearing that family may hear*) Then we took a lot of cigarettes and... things and kept going along the beach road till nearly sunrise. That's when I made that silly bet with Tobyns that I could outswim him. Oh, anything is possible on a night like that. What were you doing?

PRECIOUS   For hours I watched it from my window—the long white shoreline and the still white endless sea. And all the little dreams I had dreamed about love, and about what a lover should be, changed.

HARRY   What had you dreamed?

PRECIOUS   (*slowly—putting it into words for the first time*) I had dreamed of great love but in a small way. But as I looked out into that mysterious light that night I began to see that great love must come to the great lover as great art comes to the artist. I don't know if I can make it plain but—I seemed to understand how everyone who ever did anything great, or ever felt a great love, must, out of yearning for it, have grown great enough to experience it.

HARRY   The next day we met. It's gloriously romantic, isn't it!

PRECIOUS   That is why I loved you. Because you came that day— and in that strange way. I think—I had no choice—

HARRY   Then to think of finding you again—here—last night. You're not afraid of anything in the world, are you?

PRECIOUS   I love you.

> LOUIS *Prince, with letters and papers, comes along the verandah to the door. His moving shadow is seen before he comes into sight.*

HARRY   You're wonderful! Last night—to love like that without a doubt or a question. How could you dare?

PRECIOUS   Last night—I heard the song of the earth.

> *LOUIS Prince appears, pauses outside the door observing them, then comes in unobserved.*

LOUIS   Boat come.

> *LOUIS gives mail to HARRY.*

HARRY   All for Father. None for me or for Miss Conroy. (*thrusts letters at LOUIS*) Father is still at breakfast.

LOUIS   (*refusing letters*) No. Much work now. You go.

> *HARRY hesitates an instance, then takes the letters and exits quickly. PRECIOUS looks at LOUIS for a moment or two, makes a move to follow HARRY, then stops short, realising that LOUIS will intercept her.*

PRECIOUS   You have work outdoors for Mr. Maclean, you need not wait.

LOUIS   (*strong "Injun" accent*) No work. I say that to boy. He goes.

> *PRECIOUS goes to statue and makes pretense of modelling.*

PRECIOUS   Why do you talk like that?

LOUIS   You speak to Louis Prince like Indian. Louis Prince answer you like Indian. (*PRECIOUS fumbles, drops her tool and turns to face him.*) Son of Maclean is your brother.

PRECIOUS   No, Mr. Harry Maclean is not my own brother.

LOUIS   (*assenting*) No.

PRECIOUS   What do you mean, Louis Prince?

LOUIS   White boy is as your brother.

PRECIOUS   (*baffled but with determined lightness picks up tools and begins to model*) Oh, that is the Indian way of looking at it?

LOUIS   Yes. (*pause*) Where is your mother, *Red Cloud?*

PRECIOUS   She is dead—long ago.

LOUIS   Yes. Where is her grave?

PRECIOUS   Her grave? Why—I do not know! They have never told me.

LOUIS   You do not know. That is true.

PRECIOUS   How strange, how terrible that I do not know. Why do you speak to me of her? What do you know of my mother?

LOUIS   What is to know? She was a woman—like you. She gave herself secretly to a white man.

> *Pause. PRECIOUS, alarmed, tries to read his face to see if he knows what has passed between her and HARRY.*

There was a woman with white blood who had many sons. One day came a daughter and those who stood by called her Ama g_oot, Making Happy, because her mother smiled when she was born. Making Happy grew up. When she was fifteen years, a white fisherman came at sunset with boats. He saw her and called her from her mother's house. Making Happy followed him along the beach into forest. Many sunsets she followed him. When her child was born she named it Hluut'ws, Precious.

PRECIOUS   My name—

LOUIS   The white man returned; and again he called Ama g_oot. She went with him in the canoe. The wind came up strongly and the canoe overturned. The white man held on to the canoe and saved himself. But Ama g_oot had no strength, for she had knelt at the paddle all night while the white man slept—he had been very drunk. Many days after, Making Happy came floating and creeping through the sea to ask burial among her people. Her mother found her in the driftwood at the river's mouth and made her a grave in the black pine that is bent and hangs over the water there, where the great canyon begins. *They* called her back through the sea and she came to sleep and wake with her kindred the forest.

PRECIOUS   Making Happy…. Why do you tell me this story?

LOUIS   She was your mother.

PRECIOUS   My mother!

LOUIS   Yes.

PRECIOUS   My mother! No. That is impossible. Someone among your people has told you this story, but it is not true. My mother…

LOUIS   Where is her grave?

PRECIOUS   They will tell me where it is! You—how could you know of *my* mother?

LOUIS   She gave herself secretly to a white man… and then death came.

PRECIOUS   Go—go away!

LOUIS   *They* called her back even through the sea.

PRECIOUS   Harry!

> *As she makes to leave LOUIS holds her wrist.*

LOUIS   Do not call him, Bisbis hl masaaa chx. You are the Woman. For you I came out of the canyon alive where I looked for death. I have learned the song of the earth because of you..

PRECIOUS   Let me go.

LOUIS   I have spoken it only for you. And you have heard it.

PRECIOUS   Yes! I have heard it! Far away from here. Down there in the south. It was not your voice I heard.

LOUIS   That is true. It is in you. For a long, long time you stayed there in the south with white women. You thought you were like those white women. But sometimes when you were all alone you listened—listened—for something.

PRECIOUS   Yes… when I was a little child. Then it passed. Now I hear it again.

LOUIS   You forgot. But *they* never forget. You think you came back because the white preacher brought you. No. You came because you must. I also. I came back.

PRECIOUS   Came back? I never was here before. No, don't say that.

LOUIS   You do not know why you came. Once, you did not know why you listened. Now you know. They called you from the south, over the sea.

PRECIOUS   No—no—

LOUIS   Far beyond the mountain the voice comes. It is not white. No white woman hears it.

PRECIOUS   No—it's all a dream; a madness. They cannot call me. I am white.

LOUIS   You lie. *(touches her breast)* It speaks to you there. And you answer. Some day soon you will go—you will go with me.

PRECIOUS   *(whispering)* Harry.

LOUIS   Bisbis hl masaaa chx, white men do not take. They beg from their women, and leave them. They do not take, and hold with death.

PRECIOUS   Let me go.

LOUIS   You are my woman. For you they wait. Soon, maybe tonight, maybe tomorrow, I take you. *(Makes to leave. HARRY's voice heard off.)* Death comes to woman who gives herself secretly to a white man. White boy, son of Maclean, comes. He is as your brother.

PRECIOUS   *(whispering)* Yes.

> Exit LOUIS, enter MACLEAN and HARRY.

MACLEAN   A great moral victory, my son.

HARRY   Yes, Father, it'll be a very good thing—of course.

MACLEAN   It means regeneration—regeneration! *(to PRECIOUS)* A letter from the Bishop, about the cause nearest to my heart. Listen. "We are now confident that your zeal has borne fruit. We have every reason to hope that the wise and righteous law you advocated for compelling marriage between white men and the Indian women they have wronged will pass the house this coming session and be placed upon the statue books." A great moral victory. I shall devote my life to seeing that that law is enforced. *(exits)*

PRECIOUS   Why did you stay so long? I wanted you.

HARRY   Father was talking to me about the number of new converts among the Indians—

PRECIOUS   Don't talk of that now! Where is my mother buried?

HARRY   Your mother? Why... I don't know. What a strange thing to ask me now!

PRECIOUS   I need to know... I... you must find out for me.

HARRY   Precious—you're hysterical.

PRECIOUS   It's nothing. I—it's this place! I feel things here I never felt before. Do you think that the soul of an Indian could enter into a white woman?

HARRY   Of course not, Precious! What an idea!

PRECIOUS   Some people believe that. That souls are born again and again in different bodies.

HARRY   But that's just a heathen belief. We know better.

PRECIOUS   I wonder. Something is awake in me now, since I came here, that I never knew before. With you it's your father, his will, his thoughts, that have made you what you never wanted to be. But with me, it's something far stranger, far more terrible.

HARRY   What do you mean?

PRECIOUS   It is the sinister will of that great gloom out there— calling me, drawing me, and I am afraid. Take me away, Harry.

HARRY   Why, how can I?

PRECIOUS   You will, if you love me. Oh you do love me, don't you?

HARRY   I'm mad about you. I don't know myself any longer. That is love... I suppose.

PRECIOUS   You suppose? Don't you know?

HARRY   It's so different, so different from all one's ideas. Oh Precious, we—I—have done very wrong. I have wronged you, too. You must feel it so.

PRECIOUS   Wronged me? How?

HARRY   But I will marry you at once.

PRECIOUS   How can you say it in that way? Have I asked you for anything but love? When you asked me, did I wait to bargain before I gave it?

HARRY   No—no indeed. You almost make me see it as you do when you talk to me. There's something so strong, so splendid about you, Precious. It was that I felt first when you sprang into the water so fearlessly. It was just as if you were another wave of the sea, but stronger, and more compelling than the other waves. So you took me from them and carried me ashore; and then when I saw you on the beach with your red hair, falling like loose bits of sunset round you, there was the same vigour and power. I've always remembered you in that way...

PRECIOUS   Oh you do love me.

HARRY   And then last night when you stood there under the trees, something swept over me again, the great wave of you... and I...

PRECIOUS   Are you sorry?

HARRY   (*crushing her in his arms*) No! No! But you... it was all so sudden. Oh, how can you be so sure that it is love?

PRECIOUS   I know. When love comes like that... in one moment... when you've never cared for anyone before, even though you've felt something stir in you that seemed like love, yet you knew it wasn't because it couldn't speak to the whole of you; when you've felt and known all that in loneliness, with your heart starved and crying for love, and would not give up to it, but waited for the one great love that would find you at last—do you think you can make any mistake when the *one love* comes?

HARRY   Precious!

   Long embrace. Enter MRS. MACLEAN.

MRS. MACLEAN   Harry! Harry! (*They jump apart with a start. She speaks to PRECIOUS.*) I am astounded at you! What do you mean by such behaviour?

PRECIOUS   (*holding HARRY's hand*) Tell her, Harry.

HARRY   Mother, I know you are surprised and of course... Mother, I am going to marry Precious.

PRECIOUS   (*goes to MRS. MACLEAN and throws her arms around her neck*) Lallie, I'm so happy. Oh, do be pleased with us.

MRS. MACLEAN   (*throwing off PRECIOUS' embrace, to HARRY*) You are mad! You...

HARRY   I know you and Father had other plans for me, but I…
I can't marry Cissie now, Mother, because I am going to marry
Precious!

PRECIOUS   Lallie, we love each other.

MRS. MACLEAN   Love! What has that to do with it? I tell you it
can never be! My son married to you!

PRECIOUS   Lallie, why not to me? What is there wrong with me?

MRS. MACLEAN   I don't care to talk to you about it. This is
between me and my son. Harry, you must give up this ridiculous
notion. I forbid it—and so will your father.

HARRY   It's quite useless, Mother. I have made up my mind. Why
can't I marry Precious?

MRS. MACLEAN   Because her mother was a half-breed! (*to
PRECIOUS*) Now you know it.

MACLEAN enters and stands in doorway.

HARRY   What are you saying?

PRECIOUS   It's not true, Harry. It's not true.

MRS. MACLEAN   It *is* true. You have Indian blood in you.

PRECIOUS   Indian blood—no—no. Don't believe it, Harry. It's a lie!
A lie!

MACLEAN   Martha, what is happening here?

MRS. MACLEAN   He says he is going to marry Precious! With that
blood in her, and now I've told him why he can't. I've told him.

MACLEAN   Harry, what new folly is this?

HARRY   There must be some mistake, Father…

MRS. MACLEAN   Mistake! It sticks out all over her. Haven't
we seen it, your father and I, since she came back? It shows
in everything she does, everything she says. Her way of sitting,
moving, her walk, her very thoughts are Indian. Look at her
dress—

PRECIOUS   Don't say that! You don't know what you're doing.

MRS. MACLEAN   You said yesterday that you remembered your mother's face. You said it was a brown face bending over you. Well, so it was. Why, you were born there, in that village among those…. You are one of them.

PRECIOUS   No—

MRS. MACLEAN   You like to go there. You like to be among them. You say that you have "an instinct for the trail." You go off alone into the woods like an Indian. You say that you hear the woods "call you"—

PRECIOUS   No, no! I do not hear them. I said it, perhaps. But it's not true. I do not hear them.

MRS. MACLEAN   Why shouldn't you! It's in your blood! You're Indian all through.

PRECIOUS   (*holding out her arms to HARRY*) No. No! Harry—look. Look! They're white—white. And my hair—it isn't even brown, and lots of white people have brown hair. But mine isn't. You said it was like sunset just a moment ago. And my hands—you said they were like white wings. Oh, look at them again, look at me. I'm just the same as I was before you heard these things. I'm just the same.

HARRY   I won't let it make any difference—I can't now. (*takes her hands*)

MRS. MACLEAN   You insolent—you… you…! How dare you stand there with your arms around my son? Stand away from him, you…

She seems about to tear them apart. PRECIOUS faces her with rage. It stops MRS. MACLEAN.

HARRY   Mother!

PRECIOUS   Go back! Don't touch me. It will not be good for anyone who tries to step in-between Harry and me.

MACLEAN   Martha, sit down! You—er—complicate matters. I will deal with this question—on higher grounds.

MRS. MACLEAN sits down.

HARRY   Father, I must marry Precious.

MRS. MACLEAN   Marry Precious. Precious!

PRECIOUS   My name—it was you who gave it to me? (*pleading*)
You called me that.

MRS. MACLEAN   It was your mother who named you.

PRECIOUS   (*moans*) Oh—my mother.

MRS. MACLEAN   She called you Hluut'ws. It means Precious. If
she hadn't had you baptised—we would have changed the name.
It was a ridiculous name for a white girl. But, of course, you're
not white.

PRECIOUS   An Indian name. I thought that under all your coldness
you loved me. That once, when I was little, you took me to your
home because you loved me and called me Precious.

MACLEAN   Where have we failed in our self-imposed duty towards
you? You might have been an ignorant squaw wallowing in
superstition and immorality like your mother—

PRECIOUS   My mother—Making Happy—oh—don't.

MACLEAN   Or you might have been a blaspheming renegade like
your father. We have instructed you in virtue. We have taught
you to know God, the universal Father full of loving kindness.

PRECIOUS   Yes! Red and White, they are all God's children! Oh,
I've heard you say that! To those poor fools out there. To me. To
ME! Lies—lies—lies—all of it! Oh yes we are God's children so
long as we stay far away from you—you whites!

MRS. MACLEAN   Shameless girl—be silent!

PRECIOUS   But when I ask you for my share of God, for love, for
freedom to love—my birthright as well as yours! Then you cast
me out. You and your creed and your morals—why do you mock
us with lies? Why don't you leave us alone? You—make us suffer,
but you cannot make us afraid; and so you—hate us! Yes, you
hate us, because you cannot take our freedom from us, because
you can never make us like you. Because we will love and live
and be as the Earth made us!

MACLEAN   This is your gratitude! Your rebellious—I may say
heathen—spirit has turned to evil all the good things we provided
for you.

HARRY   Oh Father—no. Precious is not bad—I feel sure—

MACLEAN   The roots of sin are in her. She shows me today all the lawlessness of the untutored savage.

PRECIOUS   Lawless! Savage! Why? Because I love your son. That is my sin. I am an Indian and I love your son. And he loves me. He loves me.

MACLEAN   It is a lawless love.

PRECIOUS   It is love!

MACLEAN   If you loved him you would give him up.

PRECIOUS   No—No! I would not. I will not. I can't. I love him. Love is not for giving up. It is for holding—keeping; for happiness. It is the only thing in the world worth having—the only thing. Once and for all, I'll never give him up.

MACLEAN   That is your last word? Then hear mine. You shall never marry my son. You shall not blast his life. You shall not cause society to shut its doors against him because of you. You must leave this house at once.

PRECIOUS   Take care!

HARRY   Father, you don't know what you're doing!

PRECIOUS   *(to MACLEAN)* I will not go.

MACLEAN   Go and prepare for your journey.

PRECIOUS   If I go, he goes with me.

MRS. MACLEAN   Oh!

MACLEAN   What! You dare!

PRECIOUS   You can't separate us. It has gone too far between us. Now do you understand?

MACLEAN   What do you mean?

HARRY   Precious, I forbid you.

MRS. MACLEAN   *(simultaneously)* Robert, don't ask!

MACLEAN   What do you mean?

PRECIOUS   You know what I mean. You have been working to get a law passed to make white men marry the Indian woman they have taken. Well, I am one of those women. Now will you try to send me away?

MACLEAN   You shall go if I have to drag you by force. You wanton! You think you shall stay here under my roof to compass the destruction of my son—

PRECIOUS   I am his wife—under your law. I am his wife!

MACLEAN   That law is not yet a law.

PRECIOUS   Oh—

MACLEAN   Ay, and if it were, it would not touch my son. He is outside the laws of man. He is a minister of God. Shall I yield him up to you to destroy him? No! He is consecrated unto God. Render unto Caesar the things that are Caesar's and unto God the things that are God's.

PRECIOUS   Hypocrite.

MACLEAN   But you—whom I took from among the heathen. Your soul is black with the unpardonable sin. You have reverted to the godless ways of your Indian mother. You are no white woman.

PRECIOUS   Don't say that—

MACLEAN   Leave my house. You have no longer any right in a Christian home. (*pointing but not looking out to woods*) Go back to your mother's people! There is your place—there—where your lawless blood calls you—there!

HARRY   Father!

PRECIOUS   No, no! (*pleadingly*) Harry! (*She goes to HARRY and falls at his feet.*) Harry!

Act IV

*Late afternoon of the same day. A part of the forest on the
high bank of the river above the cannery where the great
canyon begins. As the scene progresses the light changes
from a rosy hue to a strong orange sunset, then to black
clouded dusk.*

LOUIS (*entering*) They say no have boat. All boat go far—catch
fish.

MACLEAN Miss Conroy must catch the steamer at Port Mellatchy
tomorrow. I need a boat.

LOUIS I have canoe. Strong wind coming from North. Good wind.
With some sail, it can beat any boat they got.

MACLEAN I would prefer a boat. But—if it's the only thing... very
well. Prince, you will have to take Miss Conroy in your canoe.

LOUIS Yes.

MACLEAN You will take great care of her—I can trust you?

LOUIS Yes.

MACLEAN Very well. Bring your canoe to the wharf at seven
o'clock. (*starts down the path to the cannery as LOUIS exits*)

MRS. MACLEAN (*enters, calling*) Robert.

MACLEAN comes back to meet her.

MACLEAN Martha, what is it?

MRS. MACLEAN I hurried so. Robert, I wouldn't say this in front
of others—but even you can make mistakes. You're making
a mistake now. You mustn't send that girl away.

MACLEAN When I ordered her out of my house this morning
I was overpowered by my anger. Since then, I have thought about
it calmly. I shan't thrust her out to be an influence for corruption
among my flock. She shall return to California.

MRS. MACLEAN How like a man! You only see one side of
things. You don't seem to see what may happen. There might
be a dreadful scandal—and it would all get into the papers.

MACLEAN   Oh, the papers.

MRS. MACLEAN   You never can tell how people will look at such things. They might even blame us. It is your duty as a Minister to prevent that. And Great-Aunt Eliza—what if it came to her ears? It would be the ruination of Harry!

MACLEAN   What do you suggest?

MRS. MACLEAN   Send Harry to Victoria tonight. Keep the girl with us until—if need be—we can take her away somewhere. At any rate, we can keep the matter quiet, and no-one here will blame us for anything.

MACLEAN   Harold has not shown himself fit for a serious charge.

MRS. MACLEAN   We can't stop to think about that now! I dare say he's as fit as a lot of others. You know how Harry is. He is entirely influenced by the people he's with. Once there, among new friends, in the work, all this will pass from his mind. A little later his marriage with Cissie can take place naturally.

MACLEAN   Yes… yes. I believe you are right. Tell Harry to get ready to leave right away.

> *SIM'OOGIT enters, followed by Koksilah, with baby. She sits on the ground during the following, listening intently to her husband's discussion with MACLEAN.*

MRS. MACLEAN   I must hurry back. You don't know what that girl may be doing. *(exits)*

MACLEAN   *(as he makes to exit)* Good afternoon, Sim'oogit.

SIM'OOGIT   Greetings, I would like to talk with you.

MACLEAN   Oh? I am in a hurry but, well, yes. What did you want to talk to me about?

SIM'OOGIT   You have worked much bad medicine in my village and among my people. You have told them a story of a man your tribe killed and then buried. But because your people did not walk three times around his grave shouting, his spirit was not afraid and so returned. So now you make offerings to it in fear. My people are like children, afraid of shadows. You have not done well, white man, to tell them this story.

Left to right: Beverley Machelle (Koksilah), *Duane Howard* (Sim'oogit)
photo by *Christopher LeMay*

MACLEAN   What I have told them is true, Sim'oogit. If your people
   believe it they may see the light which does not die.

SIM'OOGIT   Wah! You lie. There is but one light that does not die.
   (*pointing upward*) We are people of the Light. What is your light
   to us? Bah! I have come to talk to you about my son.

MACLEAN   I'm listening.

SIM'OOGIT   Look at me, white man. I am a great chief and mighty,
   but I am old. I have borne eight sons and have seen seven grow

until their eyes looked into mine and their shoulder stood by my shoulders. In all the country there were no sons like my sons. My first born, Black Fox, was hanged by the chief of white men because, when the white fisherman took his wife, Black Fox cut out the fisherman's heart with his knife. So a great sorrow came upon me.

MACLEAN   Black Fox took the life of a man in the evil passion of revenge.

SIM'OOGIT   Did the White Chief take the life of Black Fox for the love of him? You lie, White Man, and there is no wisdom in your lies. Then the coughing sickness came and my sons fell. Five times—five times—I bowed my head and mourned. Now I have but two sons. (*points to baby in Koksilah's arms*) One is a baby and sickly. One is Hlaagoo't, Louis Prince as you call him.

MACLEAN   Louis Prince bows before the great Spirit whom I serve.

SIM'OOGIT   Yes. You have filled his heart with madness. I'm old. The Eagle waits to bear away my spirit. Who will then be Chief among my people? Louis Prince is tall and strong; as swift as a deer. He was free and mighty before you worked the spell of evil upon his Spirit. I have no more sons. The White Man's law and the White Man's death have taken six. Have I given the White Man's God enough?

MACLEAN   The God of white men—

SIM'OOGIT   I care nothing for your Gods. I am not afraid of them. But my heart is like a woman's towards Louis Prince. I know you can lift the spell you have worked upon his heart. I have much wealth. I will give you 300 skins and 900 blankets, so that you will lift the spell from my son's heart.

MACLEAN   The Great Spirit is not interested in blankets and furs.

SIM'OOGIT   Then I will give him the war canoe of Sim'oogit, the horns of slain deer and the plate of copper carved by slaves. I will give you 300 skins of the silver fox, ermine and bear, so that you will turn the heart of my son to his people once again. So that I may see Hlaagoo't a man once more before I die. Is it enough?

MACLEAN   What is given to the white man's God does not come
back again. Even if you brought me all the canoes and the copper
and blankets in the country, I would still say no.

    Koksilah stands, holding baby with outstretched arms.

SIM'OOGIT   Shall I see thy babe when he is a man? (*Koksilah sinks
down. SIM'OOGIT turns to MACLEAN.*) My heart is sick with
sorrow. Give me back my son.

MACLEAN   No, that I cannot do.... When will you worship the
God of your son?

SIM'OOGIT   (*During the following he draws his knife from sheath and
rips a piece of bark off nearby tree. He cuts his left arm and marks
a symbol on the inner bark of the tree, high up, nearly at full height
of his arm.*) Evil be upon your tribe! Evil be brought upon your
house as you have brought evil upon my house. May your heart
break before your son, as my heart breaks before Louis Prince.
May the winter of your years be lonely and forsaken. May you die
and fall into the ground and leave no son to fast above your
grave. So may your tribe die with you. O stealer of sons. (*With all
his force he plunges knife into the tree up to its hilt, steps back then
raises his arms.*) Indian curse, white man. My life is done. I wait
the coming of the eagle. (*exits followed by Koksilah*)

MACLEAN   It's astonishing how these people cling to their
superstitions. (*exits*)

    *PRECIOUS enters, LOUIS Prince's knife in her belt. Hunting
for her mother's grave, she slowly makes her way to the bent
pine where the grave is.*

PRECIOUS   Making Happy.

    HARRY enters. PRECIOUS turns and sees him.

Harry, you came to find me! And I've looked for you everywhere.

HARRY   You must have known Father was with me, till just now.
And it isn't safe for us to be seen talking together.

PRECIOUS   We must talk together and decide what we shall do.

HARRY   (*irritably*) Oh, very well. Perhaps you're right. Though
I don't know why I should be expected to have anything to say
now. You and Father have done all the talking so far. It seems to

be my part to keep quiet and have other people settle my life for me.

PRECIOUS   I only want to make you happy.... Oh!... Making Happy.

HARRY   Happy! I never expect to be happy again.

> *LOUIS Prince enters, carrying a paddle.*

LOUIS   I go. I take paddle to boat.

> *PRECIOUS turns in sharp fear and meets LOUIS' noncommittal gaze.*

HARRY   Very well. Go on, Prince. Tell Father I'll be there in a minute. Don't—er—you needn't mention...

LOUIS   *(looking at PRECIOUS)* Yes I go. Son of Maclean say farewell to Bisbis hl masaaa chx by grave of Ama g_oot. *(points to bent pine confirming PRECIOUS' intuition, then exits)*

HARRY   By the grave... what did he mean? What's the matter, Precious?

PRECIOUS   You will never say farewell to me, no matter what comes.

HARRY   Oh, I don't know. What do you suppose we can do, with Father against us?

PRECIOUS   Your father! He is not the thing to fear! That is only your old idea of his power over you. You have always given in to it. It will be like that until you get away from him entirely. When you feel that power, that something mighty is fastening itself upon you and drawing, drawing you, the only thing to do is to get away before... before it is... too late.

HARRY   You are so precipitate and unreasonable, Precious, and you don't see how much I have to worry about. It isn't as if I hadn't stood by you, through that awful scene.

PRECIOUS   Dearest. Take me away tonight, no matter where. I am strong enough to take all your troubles, if you love me. I can bear anything, everything, for you.

HARRY   Oh, Precious. I know all that. But you can't expect to settle my whole life for me. There are other things besides love to be considered.

PRECIOUS   Other things.

HARRY   Yes. And, Precious—(*CONROY, pretty drunk, comes up path unseen by HARRY and PRECIOUS.*)—Perhaps, perhaps it would be better to part. Don't look at me like that. It would break my heart, of course. I only said it might be better. Don't look at me like that—you frighten me. (*PRECIOUS has backed up stage to the bent pine. She puts her hand on it for support.*)

PRECIOUS   Don't say that—ever—again.

HARRY   I only meant—

PRECIOUS   If you should leave me—but you couldn't! You couldn't! Don't say that again—it's not a safe thing to say—not here.

HARRY   Well—what do you propose to do?

PRECIOUS   Your father has planned to send me back to California. He has hired one of the fishermen to take me to Port Mellatchy to catch the boat. I am to leave here tonight. You must go with me.

   CONROY is taking this all in.

HARRY   That's impossible! Utterly impossible! Besides no, Mother says that instead of sending you, I—

PRECIOUS   You must. I dare not stay here. I will not go without you. Oh—your father himself should marry us—now that he knows.

HARRY   Yes! "Now that he knows!" And how does he know? Because you told him. You—

PRECIOUS   Harry—

HARRY   Yes! To tell my father a thing like that! And before my mother. How could you! A thing even the worst woman of that sort tries to hide from good people.

PRECIOUS   The worst woman of that—Harry!

CONROY   (*approaching*) So that's the sort of woman you are, my girl! What's bred in the bone'll come out in the blood.

PRECIOUS   Who are you? Go away!

CONROY   And that's the sort you are! With all the churching and the schooling and the money spent on you that she wouldn't give to an honest white man and her own son. No, but she'd let that sneaking preacher have it to waste it—waste it—on a squaw brat. Oh the waste, the waste.

PRECIOUS   Harry...

HARRY   Who is he?

PRECIOUS   I don't know. Oh, make him go away.

CONROY   No you don't. Not so fast. Think I don't know you, eh? You—you that's been made a lady of. You that's been brought up in luxury while your poor old father was starving. You that's been sleeping on feathers while your lawful father had nowhere to lay his head—savin' amongst Indians and savages—savages and vermin. A white man. A white man. The pity of it. But I'll put an end to it! I'll put a stop to your wallowin' in luxuries you were never born to. I'll teach that pasty-faced parson commandments. Fish blood he has, fish blood! Fish blood and pasty face. I'll show him what comes of taking my daughter from me! I'll instruct him.

HARRY   What do you mean? Who took your daughter from you?

PRECIOUS   Don't ask. Come away.

CONROY   Your father took her—yes—that's the kind of a Christian he is! Took my own daughter from me and taught her to revile me with scorn. But the Lord's judgement has come on him for it, as I'll reveal. Yes! I'll reveal it! I'll tell him a tale. *(to PRECIOUS)* Where's your father?

PRECIOUS   He is dead. Dead!

CONROY   Dead is he? Do you know who I am, eh? Do you?

PRECIOUS   I don't want to know.

CONROY   I am your begotten father, Thomas Conroy. That's who I am.

HARRY   Is this true? What have you been hiding from me?

PRECIOUS   No, no! It's not true.

CONROY   Not legally, no. Not legally. You don't suppose Tom
Conroy would marry with an Indian, do you?

HARRY   What do you mean?

PRECIOUS   Harry—

HARRY   I will hear. If it's true—

PRECIOUS   If you were a man you'd hit him!

CONROY   So that's your tune, is it? I'll teach you to talk like that to
a white man—and your father! The father you owe the breath of
life to. Where'd you be I'd like to know if I hadn't begotten you?
Who'd have given you birth? And that's not the only sacrifice I've
made for you. No! I've given up everything in life for you—had it
all taken from me. Disinherited I was because of you and that
sneakin' parson and my lovin' Cousin Martha. Oh, they told her,
my prayin' lady mother with her moneybags—oh they told her
for a purpose! Turned her against me and got the money for their
own! And more of it for sinful wastin' on you that's the cause of
all my misfortune! You! You couldn't live honest could you? Not
with the breed you come of! Jezebel! A Babylonish woman! Out
on you! A stealin' thievin' ruination!

PRECIOUS   (*in appeal*) Harry...

HARRY   Ugh! No! (*goes to leave*)

PRECIOUS   (*screams*) Harry, don't leave me!

HARRY   I'm done! You've dragged me low enough but you shan't
ruin me. Ugh—it's revolting. I'm done. (*exits*)

CONROY   (*seizing stick from forest debris*) Women—women—
brown or white, what are they? Lustful, vain, deceivin'! Castin'
their eyes for honest men to drag them down. Serve them as
they deserve—despised creatures. Despised and rejected of men.
What's a maiden without virtue? Mockin' holy matrimony. Oh,
that I see every loose woman get her punishment! Illegal and
a breed and a Jezebel! Disinheritin' your own father. Bringin'
down his heirs with dishonour. But I've got an arm! (*He advances
toward PRECIOUS. PRECIOUS, faint and dazed with horror, seems
unable to defend herself.*) A strong arm, praise the Lord. (*LOUIS
Prince enters up the path unperceived.*) As others have found that
presumed. Rob me, will you? Dishonour a white man? Shame my

Left to right: Odessa Shuquaya (Precious), Terrence Loychuk (Conroy)
photo by Christopher LeMay

blood in you? Make my name a by-word with your goin's on? Praise the Lord, I'm your father. I'll chasten you. I'll chasten you! Harlot! Harlot!

> *CONROY raises his arm to strike PRECIOUS. LOUIS steps quickly in between the two and faces CONROY. LOUIS pushes CONROY away, quickly draws a knife and runs the blade lightly and slowly along CONROY's bare throat from ear to ear. CONROY drops the stick and grovels, sobbing.*

Don't hurt me! I'm a brother! A brother! My threat—it's my duty. It's my own flesh and blood. A father's love—redeem the lost. *(Sees Sim'oogit's curse and goes wild with terror. Points to it and shakes.)* Ah! *(LOUIS Prince deliberately pushes him up against the tree.)* I'm a brother!

> *LOUIS steps back, eyes CONROY, spits at him, then turns his back on him. (This is a deadly insult.) CONROY flees, screaming. LOUIS turns to the tree and examines the knife. Sees it's his father's, steps back and lifts his hand a full arms-length above his head. PRECIOUS is swaying and holding onto the pine. He moves towards her. She, thinking he is going to kill her, falls prone before him. He looks at her and then up at branches of the pine.*

LOUIS   Hluut'ws. *(sadly)* Death waits. White father. White friends. White lover throw you away! You fall like a dead bird in the white winter. They throw you back to earth. You lie on the ground at Indian feet. You, Bisbis hl masaaa chx, Light-bringer, my Woman.

PRECIOUS   I was white too. White, like them. Like them.

LOUIS   That was your dream. How could you be like them? There were earth voices in you.

PRECIOUS   Yes.

LOUIS   Bisbis hl masaaa chx, with hair that was like young morning. Your face lifted high to shine across the dark. Now you sink to the earth like the end of the day. To love you—that was *my* dream. To desire you was as light coming over a great sea. For you I could wait as these cliffs wait for little flowers. You were my woman; and yet you fell under the white hand.

PRECIOUS   I—too—have white blood.

LOUIS   White blood is their blood. Father's blood; lover's blood. Their blood has betrayed you. Your eyes weep. Eyes that followed a white man. Now they see nothing for tears. The eyes of young morning are black with sorrow. The day ends, Bisbis hl masaaa chx. Life sets like sun.

PRECIOUS   There is no place for me.

LOUIS   Ancient tribal law says the woman who gives herself
secretly, not by our law, is cast out to wander alone through
forest. In one moon if there is a man who has loved her, he may
look for her to kill her if she is still alive; or to live alone with her
in the forest. No man yet has left his tribe to live in the forest
with a cast-out woman. The law says that the man who brings the
woman-sorrow on another is killed swiftly.

PRECIOUS   The man who brings the woman-sorrow on another is
killed swiftly.

LOUIS   It is a sacrifice. Yeast of the sunset, cleansing the tribe. So
the blood of sunset makes the world clean, pouring on the great
alter. Now, the law is broken. Indian woman has followed a white
man in faith, and they die. But white men go on.

PRECIOUS   I am cast out.

LOUIS   You were my woman. I had called you. The song of the
taken woman was in your breast.

PRECIOUS   I did not know it was for you.

LOUIS   (*in great grief*) You were my woman.

   The wind begins to sigh down the canyon.

PRECIOUS   The air is the wind of love
From the wings of eagles mating,
Eagles, my sky is dark with your wings.

LOUIS   Bisbis hl masaaa chx. Beloved. Was it to die for love of
a white man they called you back? Was it to pierce your heart
they sent me here saying "Where is the woman?" There is grief in
that far, far country beyond the canyon. Grief in the country of
my hope.

PRECIOUS   (*stoically, understanding the law*) I am cast out to die.
You will kill me.

   *He moves toward her, bends over as if to kill her—then
   stops.*

LOUIS   I—do not know. I think "She had loved the white man" and
back into my heart comes hate, black and swift like a cloud of
wild hawks. Then I am glad for the laws of my tribe and for my
knife. The blade leaps against my thigh. The handle pushes

against me. And my hand grows strong with the old law. Then I look at you.... I look at you and still you give me light. Bisbis hl masaaa chx. Still you are Light-Bringer. The woman waited for. And my knife lies quiet again. I remember that death is the White Man's dream—and I waken. I am going to go now. Maclean is waiting for the canoe. He wants the canoe to take his son to Mellatchy. He wants you to stay here in the house. I will return in two sunsets, Bisbis hl masaaa chx. And I will look for you. And... *(taking out knife again)* I do not know.... But when I see your face again I shall know. *(exits quickly)*

> *The wind rustles through the pines. Dark clouds move across the canyon.*

PRECIOUS   *(stands, looks up at branches)* Little young lonely mother. Like me—you followed him into the twilight. Kneeling at the paddle all night—labouring against the strong tide for him while he slept. Poor little wearied faithful hands—too tired to hold to life. He saved himself; and the sea swept over you. You died in the sea for him. And I—I went to the sea—for *him.* I brought him living from the sea where you died. And he leaves me. The two white men—little mother—they cast me out to die—like you. They cast me out, those white men with vile names, to wander like a lost thing till his knife finds me. Death— or—the Woman. *(sinks into squat)* Woman—(*She bows her head between her knees and wails. She raises her head and stares out. She takes her knife out of her belt and looks at it.*) A white man's dream.

> *HARRY enters in travelling attire. He does not see PRECIOUS though she sees him. She leaps up and stealthily circles round him, appearing before him to block his exit.*

HARRY   You are here again?

PRECIOUS   Yes, Harry. I am here. You are going away? Why?

HARRY   Why? As if you needed to ask!

PRECIOUS   I didn't know, Harry. They told me he was dead.

HARRY   Well, he's not.

PRECIOUS   Harry, it wouldn't matter. Nothing that has happened would matter if we were away from here. I am just what I was that day at Santa Cruz. I am not changed.

HARRY   Precious, it's of no use to talk like this. It's of no use to talk at all. Oh, you must see yourself how unsuitable it all is. Besides, now I've given my word to my father.

PRECIOUS   Last night, you gave your word to me. Why are you breaking *that* word? Why?

HARRY   It is my duty to please my father.

PRECIOUS   You didn't think so last night.

HARRY   Oh, last night! I am sick of the thought of it. Do you suppose a man wants his whole life decided like that—in a moment of madness?

PRECIOUS   I don't understand. My life was decided in the first moment that we met. And that evening when I saw you again— well—it was just what I had known must be whenever we should meet again. In that moment I knew why I had waited. It was for you.

HARRY   It was a mistake.

PRECIOUS   I loved you. I gave you all that I am. It must be yours for always. Harry, what is there left for me if you go? If I am not yours now—what am I? How could I know that it was not the same with you? It was, it was. You told me so.

HARRY   I—I—I'm awfully sorry, Precious, really I am. Please don't talk about it any more. I didn't know what I was saying.

PRECIOUS   Is it my—that man—that makes you say it's all over? Is it only that?

HARRY   Well, no! If you must know, it's—it's everything.

PRECIOUS   Be careful. I will not let you go.

HARRY   It's all over. I don't love you. Stop—listen to me. I know I've treated you badly, but it wasn't all my fault. You swept me away, and I didn't know what I was doing. I was very wrong but it can't be helped now. Still, I'm not going to make bad worse by marrying you against my father's will. I want you to go away, back to California... and if anything should happen later, I'll do all I can for you.

PRECIOUS   You'll pension me off. Bah! Do you think I would thank you for that? Do you think I would take anything from you but love and the right to love you? I'm no coward. I could carry your child in my arms through want and disgrace with my heart singing like a thousand birds so long as you were true. But you cannot take me—and cast me off—and go on.

HARRY   You have no choice. I don't love you, I never loved you. It is just as my father said. You don't understand our way of looking at things.

PRECIOUS   No, yours is the white way! And I'm Indian... Indian.

> *LOUIS Prince enters unseen.*

HARRY   Yes! And I've done with you. Now do you understand?

> *He tries to pass. She moves swiftly upon him. He retreats until he is close to the tree with Sim'oogit's curse on it, his back to it.*

PRECIOUS   You shan't go.

HARRY   I will. I tell you my life is my own.

PRECIOUS   No.

> *She springs forward and stabs him. Same picture as when Sim'oogit stabbed the tree. HARRY falls to the ground, dead. She looks up into her mother's pine then sinks down sobbing, the knife falling from her grasp. LOUIS approaches swiftly and takes her up in his arms.*

LOUIS   (*as she droops on his arm*) A white man's dream. (*PRECIOUS seems to gain strength from him and slowly stands up straight beside him. LOUIS looks at her, comes to a decision, then points toward the mountains.*) They wait. Come.

> *He points to the paddle. She picks it up after an instant's wait. He strides off. She stands aside instinctively to let him pass. As he passes her he makes a gesture of command and goes on. She follows him submissively down the trail as...*

(*voiceover*) But Kalista heard a voice speaking from afar: "I will be a mighty hunter in a country of my own.... And Yagoot, the swift and white was his. And he found that the dream was true and Kalista lives forever in his mountain with Yagoot."

> *Curtain.*

Translations
Gitxsan Words, Names and Phrases

Sim'oogit	=	Chief
Hlaagoo't	=	Brave Heart
Ama g_oot	=	Making Happy. [literally "good hearted"]
Hluut'ws	=	Precious
Bisbis hl masaaa chx (Louis Prince's name for Precious)	=	Dawn [literally "ripping open the night"]
Gala nax_ nitswin ahl algax_hl naks'y gohl wilp ama dalxasxw	=	Come hear the words of her husband when he makes his medicine in the little white house.
*Hen ahl amstwaa Sim'oogit wa'y needi'n didalk_ lok'm x_aak_*	=	Tell the white woman that I am Sim'oogit. Sim'oogit talks not with... [a derogatory name for a woman—literally: "rotten foam that boils up when boiling wild meat."]
nox	=	mother

Afterword
"Blood will tell"
Interracial Ideologies and Racial Hybridity in *Birthright*
by Michelle La Flamme

My own research into racial hybridity deals with the following set of questions: What are the complex signifiers associated with the soma text of the racially hybrid body on stage in Canada? [1] What is the relationship between the audience and the racialised body (performer) on stage? What is the audience witnessing and participating in when viewing the racially hybrid body on stage? How does the staging of race in contemporary Canadian theatre differ from earlier performances of racially hybrid identities on stage?

The presentation of a racially hybrid body on stage may reinforce essentialist blood-quantum paradigms, deconstruct or reinforce third space paradigms, become a metaphor for interracial alliances and/or present some complicated issues around casting and audience-actor looking relations. By looking at the play *Birthright*, I will explore: 1) the character's embodiment of racial hybridity and the ideological ramifications of this complex somatic signifier; 2) the ways in which racial hybridity contributes to the ironic revelations that form the core of the dramatic structure in this narrative; 3) how this play uses the trope of the racially hybrid body as a metaphor for interraciality in Canada.

The play *Birthright*, written in 1905 by Constance Lindsay Skinner, is one of the most important early Canadian plays to address racial hybridity. Unfortunately, the developing field of critical mixed-race studies in Canada has not taken this play into consideration and it has been completely obscured in Canadian literary studies. It is an important play for the purposes of my own research because it is an early example of a Canadian play that deals with the phenomenon of a racially mixed character who specifically addresses her own biracial subjectivity within the narrative rather than simply appearing on stage as trope for interraciality. [2]

In *Birthright* both the dramatic revelations and irony are founded on the racial hybridity of Precious, the central half-breed character. The play represents differing views towards interraciality and foregrounding half-breed characters. The racially hybrid soma text signifies the ideologies around interracial unions between Native and non-Native people in Canada while simultaneously signifying the fear of miscegenation that is the subtext for the play as a whole. [3] The play explores and exposes some of the myths of Canadian nationhood through its exploration of interracial issues and Native-white relations. [4] *Birthright* deals with the issues of interraciality between Native and non-Native people in early Canadian history in a way that re-imagines the Canadian nation by way of interraciality between Native and non-Native characters.

Early staging of racial hybridity in Canada may be understood as a frame for analysing contemporary representations of racial hybridity in Canadian theatre. While *Birthright* is an early example of racial hybridity being dramatised, the most prominent early Canadian figure who literally and figuratively represented racial hybridity through her own autobiographical voice on stage is the poet/performer Pauline Johnson. [5] Johnson was the first racially-mixed Native woman in Canada to gain fame for successfully performing her dual racial heritage on stage. She also wrote about her dual racial identity in the late nineteenth and early twentieth century. [6] For these reasons, Johnson is an important historical figure for the study of the theatrical staging of racial hybridity in Canada. [7] Johnson's performances, like the play *Birthright*, suggest the centrality of interracial alliances in early Canadian history and an early twentieth century interest in issues of interraciality.

Although the play is dated, the issues it raises are contemporary and can be found in other Canadian plays that represent the racially hybrid character on stage. [8] Many of the themes that are central to mixed-race narratives are represented in this play: the warring blood hypothesis, an appeal to an essential notion of racial identity, the tragic mixed-blood paradigm, secrets and shame about interracial alliances, and cross-cultural tensions between Native and non-Native communities. These tensions are signified by the corporeality of the central character's soma text in *Birthright*. [9] I will now take some time to trace the racial ideologies inherent in this play in order to argue that this play is important for analysing dramatic representations of racial hybridity in Canada.

Tensions between Native and non-Native communities, including the attraction between Native and non-Native people are addressed throughout the play. The play foregrounds the intergenerational effects of interracial relations in Canada and numerous reactions to racial amalgamation through the racial ideologies represented by each and every character. In this way, Skinner uses the play *Birthright* to represent a range of views towards interracial unions in Canada.

Mr. Maclean initially represents a progressive view towards racial amalgamation. In the play, he attempts to pass legislation that will require white men to marry their "country brides." In Canadian history many Native women were taken as "country brides" by white European men and then summarily discarded when European women became available. Mr. Maclean describes his "mission to Ottawa" which is to "urge that some law be passed compelling all men [...] aimed principally at white men who have [...] taken up their abode with native women or the descendants of native women, to marry these women legally and through the church" (8). Mr. Maclean declares that he will "devote [his] life to seeing that that law is enforced" (47). Although his interest in legalising these alliances is based on his strict religious views, nonetheless he represents a progressive view on interraciality.

Although Mr. Maclean's stated political and religious views on amalgamation are progressive, he panics when he discovers that his own son Harry wishes to marry their adopted half-breed daughter Precious. Precious herself challenges Mr. Maclean's hypocrisy by stating: "You have been working to get a law passed to make white men marry the Indian woman they have taken. Well, I am one of those women. Now will you try to send me away?" (54). Mr. Maclean argues that Precious' "soul is black with unpardonable sin" because she has taken up with Harry. Her interracial desire suggests to Mr. Maclean that she has "reverted to the godless ways of [her] Indian mother" (54). With this announcement he throws Precious from his house, points to the woods and tells her: "Go back to your mother's people! There is your place—there—where your lawless blood calls you—there!" (54). Mr. Maclean reads Precious' "lawlessness" as a symptom of her savage Native blood. Despite his stated interest in legalising interracial unions, Mr. Maclean's prohibition of his son's desire to marry a half-breed woman represents an essentialist view of blood and the racial ideology that the races should not "mix."

Mrs. Maclean represents the liberal Canadian view that white people should help the "poor natives." Her smug attitude of superiority is also exposed in the play because when she is faced with the prospect of her son marrying Precious she also panics and refers to the idea of Precious marrying her son Harry as "utterly impossible!" and "[a]trocious" (21) "[b]ecause her mother was a half-breed" (50). Throughout the first half of the play Mrs. Maclean is shown as a character who carries a lot of shame about Precious' "wild blood." Although Mrs. Maclean evokes some empathy in her desire to "save" the half-breed character from further downfall, her hypocrisy is also revealed in her real motive, which is to save her son and her family from an interracial scandal.

Precious is read by Mrs. Maclean as being unconventional in her manner, her clothing, her art, and her views about nature, religion and Native people. Mrs. Maclean states that her Native blood "shows in everything she does, everything she says. Her way of sitting, moving, her walk, her very thoughts are Indian [...] her dress" (50). The ideology that Mrs. Maclean represents suggests that there is something inherently degenerate in Native blood that will eventually reveal itself and the idea that the presence of Native blood disables one from claiming a white identity.

Mrs. Maclean declares that Precious is not white despite her white soma text. In Mrs. Maclean's view, because Precious has the taint of Native blood, she will forever be read as non-white. Mr. Maclean also reads her soma text as indelibly Native despite her mixedness when he tells Precious: "You are no white woman" (54). The Macleans represent the ideology that one's blood is the most important determinant for one's racial identity and the ideology that "one drop" will make a racially-hybrid person non-white. [10] Mrs. Redfern and her daughter Cissie reveal their racist belief in the superiority of white people but their racism is not hidden behind saviour complexes like Mrs. Maclean, or religious hypocrisy like Mr. Maclean.

The Native characters also represent a belief in the inherent superiority of *their* blood. The Native chief, Sim'oogit states to his son Louis Prince, "I did wrong when I mated with the white blood of your mother, for now I have a son whose spirit is like that of the weasel and whose heart is foolish"(27). Exogamy is prohibited mythically and culturally in this play. The Native father frames this racial ideology within a traditional notion that curses will be exacted on a woman who has had sex with a white man. Louis Prince reveals the story of his mother "The Wind-Promise" who birthed five children, four of whom died. The play suggests that this was the curse that Sim'oogit brought upon himself by sleeping with the white blood of "The Wind Promise."

Precious is also understood by the Native characters as being cursed because both she and her mother have slept with white men. Interracial alliances are represented from the perspective of the Native characters who fear and oppose the notion of white-Native sexual unions.

It is rare for a Canadian play written by a non-Native person to foreground the many ways in which mythological and personal notions of contamination are framed within a Native perspective. The white and Native characters in this play express the *same* fear of exogamy through the racial ideology that blood must remain pure and untainted by the presence of different races. In the course of the play it becomes evident that the Macleans wish to save their son from the taint of Precious' Native blood. For the Native characters in the play, contact with white people also interestingly signifies contamination. Skinner presents a parallel storyline by representing Sim'oogit's desire to "save" his son Louis Prince and his community from the poison of the white man and the Macleans' desire to save their son form the "taint" of Native blood. These essentialist beliefs are reinforced in the play by representing these ideologies from both Native and non-Native perspectives as the central motive for prohibiting interracial unions.

Despite these prohibitions against interracial sexual unions, at the centre of the play is a love triangle between Precious, Louis (the mixed-race Native man who has saved her from being consumed by a bear) and Harry, the white man whom she has saved from drowning. The story of Cissie Redfern, the white debutante who has been promised to Harry, is secondary in the play because Skinner chooses to focus on the much more complex trajectories that result from the interracial love triangle. Both Harry and Louis declare their love for Precious and suggest that she is "the only woman" for them. Harry does so because he assumes Precious is white but Louis does so because he knows she is a "half-breed" like himself. Harry's stated "love" for Precious is challenged when she is revealed to be part Native and therefore, according to his white family, she is totally unsuitable for a bride.

When Harry retracts his interest in Precious the play becomes a half-breed romance. It is rare to see a play that features two Native half-breed characters expressing intimacy towards one another. [11] Precious is linked to Louis Prince because they are both half-breeds, both have been educated in the white world and because they are both artists. This young Native son is celebrated by the white community when he plays the violin in Montreal and is simultaneously rejected for being Indian. [12] So too, is Precious sent away to become educated and then her art is rejected by the Macleans as unsuitable. The most moving scene in the play exists when Precious and Louis hold one another and express respect, intimacy and a rather essentialist "innate" link to nature due to a naturalised "call" that has brought them together. For all its maudlin sentimentalism, the expression of love and intimacy between two Native characters on stage is rare. [13] By shifting the narrative from the interracial love triangle to a half-breed romance, Skinner seems to be suggesting that all racial groups must keep to their own "kind" rather than attempt to cross racial lines.

Racial lines are also addressed through the soma text of Precious in the form of a passing narrative. The central focus of the play is on the half-breed bastard child Precious Conroy who has been successfully "passing" as white. Precious herself is the result of an interracial relationship between her Native mother and white father. The central irony in the play is that Precious is unaware of her Native blood and is thus unknowingly "passing" as a white woman. Because her soma text is white and she has red hair, she is "read" as white by Harry who falls madly in love with her. Ironically, Precious' soma text is read as white by Harry and Native by Louis, making for the central mis-recognition of her identity due to her complex and ambiguous soma text. Louis expresses his interest in Precious as something that is based on her near white soma text. He states "I have te heart on fire for woman wit te face like white waters and te hair like red cloud"(19). Through a series of revelations Precious becomes aware of the racial identity of her birth parents and her own mixed-race lineage. The play reveals that Precious prefers "the Indian dress quite naturally" and also that she feels the "call" of nature. These essentialist beliefs inform the play's racial ideologies and support the idea that Native blood will reveal itself over the course of time despite one's ability to "pass" temporarily as white.

Skinner challenges a straightforward essentialist notion of blood as the main determinant for one's character by developing three aspects of Precious' character that suggest her actions stem from her artistic impulses, her feminist belief in her right to love whom she chooses, and the presence of her indigenous blood. Like Emily Carr, Precious feels an affinity to the natural world. Her interest in creating nude sculptures and defiant insistence that she, as an artist, should have freedom to express herself, is part of her unconventional behaviour. Precious asserts her right to follow her heart and this is a very unconventional representation of a woman, especially at the turn of the century.

Precious is represented in the play as being unconventional and we, as audience members, wonder if she is unconventional because of her education as an artist, her romantic sensibilities or the presence of her wayward and demented Native blood.

The power dynamics between men and women, Native and non-Native, are informed by gender in this play. Reverend Father Maclean is the overlord of the women in his household. His patriarchal attitude towards women is also echoed in Louis' desire to claim Precious as "his woman" and Harry's interest in "taking her" in the woods. Louis frames this desire within a Native mythological notion of the inherent rightness of he and Precious being "called" together. Women's lives and bodies are repeatedly framed throughout this play by Native and non-Native patriarchal ideals. Despite these patriarchal investments, the play is refreshing in its depiction of an early feminist character who struggles to claim what she sees as her "birthright"; the right to love whom she chooses.

In addition, the gender dynamics of the play foreground the ways in which Native women are both objects of lust and simultaneously despised in Canada. This patriarchy is also racialised in Skinner's play. Mr. Conroy is revealed as a racist who wishes to use Precious to further his own ends. Louis explains that "white men do not take. They beg from their women, and leave them. They do not take, and hold with death" (47). In this respect, the play borrows freely from the "Pocahontas Perplex" in that Precious' "squaw" Mother, we are told, risked her life and the life of her child to "save" her drunken, white, racist husband. [14] This action sets in motion a series of events that the Native characters interpret as resulting from an intergenerational curse stemming from "laying with a white man." The "Native woman-as-saviour" narrative is extended to the half-breed daughter Precious who also seeks to save Harry from his power-hungry father, and literally saves Harry from drowning, only to be rejected yet again. If this play suggests one thing it is to be wary of Canadian white people who lust after the Native Other only to despise and reject them once they satisfy their lust. While I am a fan of exogamy, it is important to produce and circulate art that hints at the ways in which these Native-white alliances have been fraught with hypocrisy, shame and ultimately rejection for the Native person in the interracial duad. In this way the play racialises the patriarchal investment by documenting some of the ways in which interracial relations can have specific consequences for women of colour in Canada. [15]

The tragedy in the play turns on the revelations of Precious' identity and her inability to "pass" as white which, in the end, leads to her downfall. Louis Prince reveals the identity of Precious' mother, (Ama g_oot) Making Happy, who is described as a Native woman "with white blood" (45). The intergenerational interraciality is represented here by Louis who claims that Making Happy, like Precious, "gave herself secretly to a white man" (45) and therefore Making Happy and Precious are both cursed because of their sexual contact with white men.

In *Birthright* Precious does what mixed-race characters often do in "passing narratives." Typically, after the revelation of her "savage blood" the half-breed or mulatta character kills herself or is exiled. [16] Precious, as a half-breed female character, follows the usual narrative trajectory. *Birthright* takes up part of this tragic narrative in the denouement where the "mixed up half-breed" woman is cast out, suffers humiliation from everyone in the play, is threatened with physical abuse, despised, cursed, reviled and threatened with a life of wandering in the wilderness and inevitably death. Even her mixed- blood lover reviles her for being "spoiled" and contaminated by the white lover who he rightly assumes has "taken" her already.

This Canadian Native "half-breed tragedy" has, as its American counterpart, the "tragic mulatto narrative." Both forms are essentially origin stories that explore "passing" narratives and most often end in tragedy. [17] Perhaps the most radical revision to the "tragic half-breed" narrative occurs in this play in terms of the way Precious deals with her rage at being used, "spoiled" and rejected by her white lover. Her own investment in whiteness prohibits Precious from seeing through Harry's deception. Ironically, her feminist belief in her "birthright" to love whom she chooses marks her tragic downfall. However, the agency she represents through killing the white man is something new and refreshing for a dramatic narrative that features a "half-breed" woman character. [18] Such an act of defiance and rage reconfigures the notion of the passive woman and/or the passive Native woman while simultaneously suggesting that the "lawless" Native blood coursing through Precious has caused her to revert to her savage ways.

The play suggests that a larger national tragedy in Canada is the damaging effect that contact has had on Native people in Canada. In this respect sexual contact between Native and white people becomes a metaphor for colonial contact. The play signifies the historical relationship between Native women and European men during early Canadian history—a history that has been largely obscured. Half-breed women have been used by white men in Canada and rejected by white Canadian society and Precious stands in for this larger tragedy. In addition, the Native father's grief over his five dead sons, lost as a result of contact, is a part of the national blues aesthetic that informs this play.

Many of the tensions in Native/non-Native relationships are deftly sketched making this play an important narrative for all Canadians to read and/or witness in production. Although this play has much in common with the American "tragic mulatto" narrative, the half-breed characters are given some agency. It is unusual to witness a play that represents a Native character consciously playing the fool in order to mock the very people who "race" him as savage and ignorant. Most of the characters' broken English appear embarrassingly politically incorrect for modern audiences. However, there is a more subversive message here in terms of Louis' conscious manipulation of linguistic codes by choosing to play "the dumb Indian" in front of the white people all the while knowing his college education places him as intellectually superior to the whites in this small, backward town. Thus, he deliberately "dumbs down" and uses discourse that will make him appear much less intelligent to white people. This subversive code switching suggests Louis' resistance to assimilation and his own agency.

Critical mixed-race studies in Canada will need to address both Pauline Johnson and the play *Birthright* as early Canadian narratives that address racial hybridity. Johnson's representation of racial hybridity brought the corporeality of a mixed-race soma text to the Canadian stage and, unlike Skinner's tragic half-breed portrait of Precious, Johnson presented a form of biraciality that gained power from both of her European and Native lineages. Johnson's body, like the body of Precious Conroy, may be understood as the ultimate post-colonial text signifying the moment of "contact" when Native and European cultures and bloodlines became syncretically fused.

In Skinner's play racial hybridity is a trope for Canadian interraciality. If we assess the differences between the representation of racial hybridity in *Birthright* written by a monoracially identified woman in 1905 and Pauline Johnson's performances early 20th century, we can see a shift from the racially mixed character as object to the racially mixed playwright as subject in her own autobiographical discourse on racial hybridity. Johnson's work and her performances of racial hybridity in particular begin to hint at the complexities involved in the process of racialisation for half-breed Canadian women. Autobiographical representations of racial hybridity in drama did not occur with any frequency in Canada until the late 20th century when mixed-race Canadian playwrights began to reconfigure the tragic mixed-blood paradigm by way of their own autobiographical voice. Contemporary Canadian playwrights use the genre of drama and the conventions of stagecraft to comment upon the role of the racialised gaze and the signifying nature of the racially hybrid body. Recent representations of racial hybridity in Canadian drama must be read in light of these earlier representations of interraciality and the racially-mixed soma text on the Canadian stage.

(February 2005)

Endnotes

[1] I have developed the concept of the "soma text" to refer to the racially hybrid body in order to draw attention to the ways in which physical markers of race such as skin tone, eye contour and bodies are racialised or given specific ideological value. Because the multiracial body often evokes the ambiguity of these markers, I prefer to use the term "soma text" rather than "skin" in order to draw attention to the complex semiotic encoding of race in many racially hybrid bodies. I consider the racially hybrid body to be a complex signifier and am particularly interested in the ambulatory and conflicted ways in which these "soma texts" are "read."

[2] It is rather curious to note that this play, which was set in British Columbia, was never produced in Canada until 2003 although it was successfully produced in the United States of America. This fact suggests that the longer historical use of racially hybrid characters in vaudeville and within abolitionist tracts hints at the longer history of interraciality in America and thus, a longer preoccupation with this literary figure in American literature.

[3] As in the "tragic mulatta" narrative, the revelation of Precious' mixed-blood status leads to her being scorned by the white lover. However, in this Canadian narrative, Precious kills her white lover rather than follow the typical spiral downward that would often lead to the tragic mixed-blood character committing suicide in American "passing" narratives.

[4] Constance Lindsay Skinner was born and raised in the frontier settlement of Quesnel and in 1899 left BC for California. She later lived in Chicago and settled in New York. Despite the centrality of the BC setting and Canadian context of the play *Birthright*, her work was never produced in Canada until this production in 2003. For more information on this obscure playwright see Jean Barman's recent publication *Constance Lindsay Skinner: Writing the Frontier* (Toronto: University of Toronto Press, 2002).

[5] One might argue that Louis Riel represents the most prominent "mixed-race" figure in Canadian history. Other plays that might usefully be read in light of *Birthright* include the play *Riel* by John Coulter (Toronto: Ryerson Press, 1962); *The Trial of Louis Riel* by John Coulter (Ottawa: Oberon Press, 1968); and, *Louis Riel: Music*

Drama in Three Acts by Mavor Moore (Floyd Chambers Foundation, 1969).

6   In *Paddling Her Own Canoe: The Time and Texts of E. Pauline Johnson* (2000), Strong-Boag and Gerson carefully research the ways in which Johnson performed her biracial heritage in the late 19th and early 20th century.

7   See chapter 3 in Strong-Boag and Gerson (2000) for a description of Johnson's increasing use of "Native" elements in her advertising and performances. This chapter also addresses the ways in which Johnson's performances coincided with the leitmotif of the Canadian New Woman.

8   Other contemporary plays that feature racial hybridity are included in my larger analysis of racial hybridity in Canadian narratives. The plays that I analyse in this larger work include Margo Kane's *Confessions of an Indian/Cowboy* (2001), Drew Hayden Taylor's *Buz'Gem Blues* (2002), *The Baby Blues* (1997) and *Boy in the Treehouse* (2002), George Elliott Clarke's libretto *Beatrice Chancy* (1999), Marty Chan's play *Mom, Dad, I'm Living with a White Girl* (2001) and two recent unpublished plays, Tasha Faye Evans' play *She Stands Still* (2004) and Lesley Ewen's play *an understanding of brown* (2002). Each of these plays represents racial hybridity and/or the threat of racial amalgamation in Canadian contexts and therefore, I believe that it is instructive to analyse these plays in relation to each other in order to understand the ways in which racial hybridity has been represented in Canada.

9   George Elliott Clarke's play *Beatrice Chancy* (1999) also is framed around the soma text of a racially-mixed woman. In this play, the racially hybrid body becomes a trope for addressing issues of interraciality and new national ideologies that hint at the history of miscegenation in Canada.

10 See Sollors for further elaboration on the legal and socio-cultural ramifications of the "one drop" rule in African-American history.

11 Precious is read as half-breed but in fact is mostly white as her mother was half-breed. This suggests that the term half-breed can be utilised to represent different percentages of Native blood.

12 Tomson Highway's novel *Kiss of the Fur Queen* (1998) also represents the idea of the Native artist performing for non-Native people.

[13] I am arguing here that *Birthright* in many ways was unique in its representation of indigenity and racial hybridity. Other research into plays that would have been written at the same time as Skinner's *Birthright* would have to be examined in detail in order to support this point.

[14] See Rayna Green's essay "The Pocahontas Perplex" for further elaboration on the "Princess-Squaw" stereotypes which have their Christian counterparts known as the "Virgin-Whore" complex.

[15] The representation of gender in early Canadian history is also addressed in Clarke's *Beatrice Chancy* and Lorena Gale's play *Angélique*. All three plays address the racialisation of women in Canada.

[16] The Canadian novel *Tay John* (1939) by Howard O'Hagan also ends with the "half-breed" character being exiled from the community. In this novel the character Tay John stands in for the crossracial tensions that existed in Western Canada as it was being "settled." More research is needed into the ways in which racially-mixed characters stand in for national crossracial tensions.

[17] See Werner Sollors' exploration of themes of interraciality, the historical and legal ramifications of the "one drop rule," and "tragic mulatto" narratives in *Neither Black nor White yet Both: Thematic Explorations of Interracial Literature* (New York: Oxford University Press, 1997).

[18] George Elliott Clarke also has his central racially-mixed character Beatrice Chancy exact revenge on a white man in *Beatrice Chancy* (1999). Lorena Gale also rewrites the "tragic mulatto" narrative by having her character Angélique in the play *Angélique* (1999) seek revenge against white people. These plays may be read together as feminist revisions of "tragic mulatto" and "tragic half-breed" narratives. Although Canadian Native playwright Marie Humber Clements does not represent a racially hybrid character in her play *The Unnatural and Accidental Women* (2001), the central Native character takes the law into her own hands by slaying her tormenter. Read together, these contemporary plays suggest that these select playwrights have broken free from the tragic narratives that have been the predominant mode of representing Native and racially hybrid characters in contemporary Canadian drama.

Biographies

photo by Pat Burkette

Jean Barman discovered the play, *The Birthright*, in the Rare Books and Manuscripts Division of the New York Public Library while researching *Constance Lindsay Skinner: Writing on the Frontier* (University of Toronto Press, 2002), which was shortlisted by the Canadian Historical Association as best book on Canadian history. Her other books have won the BC Lieutenant Governor's Medal and twice the Canadian Historical Association's prize for British Columbia history. In 2002 she was elected a Fellow of the Royal Society of Canada.

Joan Bryans has always had a love of theatre which she has increasingly been able to satisfy as her teaching of philosophy waned. Of late she has taken to directing and producing as well as acting and now has her own company, Vital Spark theatre, whose first production was her adaptation of *Birthright* in 2003. Its next production, *Two Years in Nicola*, written by Joan, about the MacQueen sisters of the Nicola Valley, will tour in the Fall of 2005.

Michelle La Flamme's (PhD [ABD]) heritage is Métis and African-Canadian. She has been teaching for more than a decade in Canada and Europe, and has been a guest lecturer in Spain, The Netherlands and Germany. Currently, she is a doctoral candidate in the English department at UBC where she also teaches in the Theatre Department and the First Nations Studies Program. Her dissertation is entitled "Living, Writing and Staging Racial Hybridity." It analyses the multiple ways in which racial hybridity is represented in contemporary Canadian autobiographies, fiction and drama. In her other life, she has worked as a performer, she writes theatre reviews for *redwire* magazine and she is working for Margo Kane's theatre company, Full Circle, in Vancouver as the Indigenous Performing Arts Alliance (IPAA) Coordinator.